THE KEY TO MENTAL HEALTH

THE KEY TO MENTAL HEALTH

The Fastest Way to Relieve
Stress, Anxiety and Depression Symptoms

Kelly Niven
Foreword by Andy Gray

Copyright 2013 Life is Now
All Rights Reserved

ALL RIGHTS RESERVED. No part of this book may be reproduced or transmitted in any form whatsoever, electronic, or mechanical, including photocopying, recording, or by any informational storage or retrieval system without express written, dated and signed permission from the author.

Contents

Foreword	1
Introduction	7
1. What's Happening to You?	**13**
Triggers	15
Resistance	20
Letting Go	31
New Beginning	37
Symptoms of Stress, Anxiety and depression	39
How You Create Your Experience	53
2. Train Your Mind	**67**
Awareness of Your Thoughts	68
Identifying Negative Thoughts	74
Letting Go of Limiting Beliefs	77
Forgiveness	82
Visualisation and Meditation	88
Gratitude	94
Affirmations	100
Diversion	105
3. Build Physical Strength	**109**
Emotions	109
Stress	116
Diet	124
Exercise	129
Rest and Relaxation	135

4. Build Self Confidence and Self Esteem — **143**
Taking Responsibility — 144
Follow Your Intuition — 152
Build a Cheerleading Team — 158
Learning to Say No — 165
Celebrate Past Successes — 167
Living a Life of Purpose — 171

5. Additional Sources of Help — **189**
Who Should You Listen To? — 189
Support to Change — 194
Sources of Further Information — 202

Appendix — **207**
Night time Tips — 208
Morning Tips — 211
Panic Attack Tips — 213
Tips for Family/Partner — 215
Success Journal — 219

Foreword

As Human Beings we have evolved to reach for a quick fix when we encounter uncomfortable experiences, thoughts and feelings. The toleration of uncertainty and discomfort is not really necessary in today's world. Most people rarely listen to the messages that the organism sends; something needs attended to. It easy to trick our bodies and minds into believing that all is well. This usually means numbing the organism through the use of prescribed or street drugs. At times the most useful thing for a human being to do for both physical and psychological health would be to pay attention to the messages that the organism sends. For example; would it not be best to explore the stress and anxiety that lie behind some stomach ulcers rather than reach for the Lanzoprasole? Would it not be best to explore the unhappiness that lies behind the excessive use of alcohol? Would it not be best to look at lifestyle balance to reduce the tension headache rather than reach for the paracetamol? Would it not be best to explore relationships, the environment and activities and their impact on feelings of depression rather than reach for the Citalopram? Would it not be best to explore the behaviours that perpetuate social anxiety rather than reach for the propanolol?

There are of course times that medication is the answer, no doubt about it, but perhaps there are times that it is not. I would suggest that raising people's awareness of the underlying issues that contribute to psychological disorder, promoting choice as regards how the manifestation of the thoughts, feelings and behaviours caused by psychological disorder are treated and helping someone to look after themselves without the need for medication whilst recovering from their problems and difficulties is an ethical path to follow. This book provides people who are seeking to overcome their problems and difficulties with a choice. The book is full of inspiration, good advice and practical exercises that can teach and enable someone to be a real friend and support to themselves during a period of distress. For me, this can only be a good thing.

Andy Gray

BABCP Accredited Cognitive Behavioural Psychotherapist.

Dear Friend

I want you to know that no matter how bad you feel you can recover. I understand how challenging it can be.

I was prone to stress and anxiety in my early twenties. When I had my Son I again suffered from stress (diagnosed as post natal depression). Only this time I couldn't get my stress levels under control and it led to extreme anxiety.

I had a baby and toddler, had recently moved home, taken optional redundancy, lost my much loved grandmother and my own mother was unwell. It spiralled out of control and hit me hard and fast.

I stopped doing normal things. I suffered panic attacks, scary anxiety symptoms and depression. Rock bottom came when I was too scared to be left home alone. At this time I also had frightening thoughts. These thoughts repulsed me.

I needed help. The good news is when you hit rock bottom the only way is up.

I then sought help from the local GP and was offered anti-depressants which I reluctantly accepted. I didn't believe this would help me to manage my life so I started to research and find ways to heal myself. I learned about the power of my mind and how to control thoughts.

After this experience I have never suffered from anxiety again.

However I continued to live a very stressful life. I worked full time, travelled extensively through out the UK, had two small children and a divorce to deal with!

I was running on adrenalin and had a break down in July 2010. I finally stopped. I needed to change. Had I openly shared my experiences at this time with medical professionals I would have been diagnosed as having schizophrenia. Fortunately I was not afraid of my experience.

I wanted to make sure that when I wrote this not only had I recovered from stress, anxiety and depression but that I am fully free from the lifestyle that created fear in my life. I can now finally say that I have found that place.

I understand the confusion that surrounds stress, anxiety and depression.

We are all individual and unique, so some things will work for some of you and some will not.

So I write to you with all of this in mind. I understand you are unique and that your needs will not be a one size fits all. You will find your way as long as you have hope. I know that even in the darkest and scariest of places that hope exists in you, even if it is small at the moment.

I want to help you to deal with the difficulties that you are experiencing on a daily basis. This is what is most debilitating. Once you are able to manage your life on a daily basis, then you can start to deal with what caused the stress in your life.

This book will help you to understand WHAT you are feeling and WHY you are feeling this way. It will provide practical and simple tools and technique to stop or drastically reduce the symptoms that you are experiencing.

I will explain to you that you are not medically ill, that you are in fact completely normal, and that you have the same symptoms as every other stress, anxiety or depression sufferer.

I have learned that life is not meant to be a struggle. I have learned to take responsibility for my own life and that every day we are free to be who we truly are.

I not only live free from anxiety, stress and depression, but I enjoy my life. I have passion for what I do, and I wake excited about the day ahead.

I have learned to live my life in the last few years, and that started by getting to know myself very well. I went from being resentful towards others including my children, to loving my life.

Has it all been plain sailing? Absolutely not! I have had many ups and downs and continue to face challenges regularly. But this is life and living.

Where you are now and where I have been, is a very dark and lonely place.

When you learn to heal yourself, and when you find the strength to turn your life around, you are left with an incredible internal power. A strength that not everyone else has! Your confidence and belief in yourself increases dramatically.

You will never be the same person again. You will be a stronger version of yourself. You will want to start living your life. Not like the way you did before. A door will open and you can choose to enter a whole new world.

A world of mystery and magic ☺ waits............. So with much love, I wish you all the very best.

Kelly

Introduction

The aim of this book is to help you remove the distressing symptoms of severe stress including anxiety and depression.

To achieve this, the book includes:
- Information and explanations
- Exercises
- Additional Resources

It will help you to:
- To recognise the symptoms of severe stress
- To understand why you experience these symptoms
- To develop coping mechanisms to deal with extreme stress
- To build self awareness and improve self confidence

Action
Like anything in life – you get out what you put in, you reap what you sow. It is the law of cause and effect. Basically, the information contained in this book is only powerful if you do something with it.

However, please to not put yourself under any further pressure. You do not need to try everything at once. The book contains a number of techniques that you can use to remove symptoms. It is important that you take action, no matter how small.

> *"Take the first step in faith. You don't have to see the whole staircase, just take the first step."*
> **Martin Luther King, Jr.**

Individuality

You are unique and your needs are specific to you. The information and exercises in this book are intended to increase your knowledge and self awareness. The ultimate goal is that you get to know yourself better and find ways to heal that fit with your individual needs.

When you are vulnerable, it can be tempting to listen to those that insist their 'method' is the best. Of course, it can be helpful and inspiring to listen to others who have successfully recovered. That is why I wrote this for you. The information here may provide some suggestions or spark ideas in you.

As the saying goes, there is more than one way to skin a cat. You are an individual and you will find your own way.

> *"To be yourself in a world that is constantly trying to make you something else is the greatest accomplishment."*
> **Ralph Waldo Emerson**

Further support

As outlined, the purpose of this book is to help you to remove the symptoms of stress, anxiety and depression. This book does not attempt to address the reasons that caused your symptoms to occur in the first place. There are two reasons for this.

Firstly, the reasons that caused the excess stress to begin with, may have been and gone, and you are left suffering from the physical and mental symptoms.

Secondly, if you are suffering from severe stress or its manifestations of anxiety or depression, the main focus is survival – getting through the day. To attempt to explore the deep emotional causes for your distress is the potential to heighten the physical and mental symptoms even further.

Consider this story of Kate.

Kate suffered from severe emotional difficulties following the birth of her son. A few years later after the death of her father, she was still struggling. She decided to go for counselling and four weeks after commencing counselling, she suffered an emotional breakdown. The floodgates had opened and she was unable to cope with the severe physical and mental symptoms that she experienced as a result of therapy. Kate stopped counselling for five months until she had the strength to continue.

This story is illustrated not to discredit therapy or counselling – far from it. It is necessary to explore the reasons that cause severe distress.

Everything happens for a reason. There are various ways to explore the causes – therapy, counselling, alternative health techniques, and variations of personal development. If you don't explore the true causes extreme stress is likely to be a repeated pattern or cycle through-out your life.

However, In order to explore the underlying cause and reasons for distress, it is necessary that you have developed coping skills to take good care of yourself. It is often difficult to explore the past and the reasons why you are the way you are. Therefore, this guide is a supplement only and compliments many of the aforementioned techniques to develop your self-awareness.

"Character cannot be developed in ease and quiet. Only through experience of trial and suffering can the soul be strengthened, ambition inspired, and success achieved."
Helen Keller

Top tips

To get the most from this book:
- Set aside suitable time
- Avoid interruptions or distractions
- Give each section your full attention
- Practice the exercises and activities

1
What's happening to you?

This will help you to:
1. Understand the natural process of growth
2. Identify the way you resist the growth process
3. Identify your physical, mental and emotional symptoms
4. Realise how you create your experience

There is an intrinsic part in all human beings to grow and develop.

That ability to grow and develop is what produces joy, health and fulfilment. It is also a natural process.

This process of growth is challenging: it's called growth for a reason. Now, you may be aware of this process. Or you may not have yet learned about the coping mechanisms that can support growth.

Hence, the purpose of this guide is to help you get through the evolving growth process.

The process...........................

4 STAGE GROWTH PROCESS

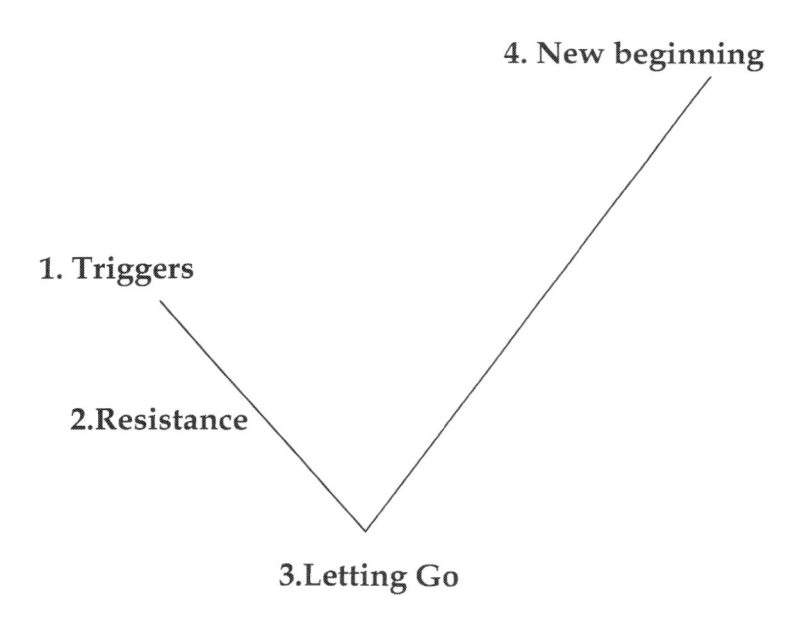

1. Triggers

2. Resistance

3. Letting Go

4. New beginning

Stage 1: Triggers

There were triggers in your life that changed your roadmap forever. You are going about your life, and something happens. Usually it's something "big" that changes the course of direction.

That something "big" is in your eyes only. What is big for you is small for me and vice versa. It is something that has a big personal emotional impact. The hard part is you don't have a crystal ball telling you what these events are going to be. There are events in life that are naturally big:

- Death
- Ill-health
- Birth
- Marriage
- Divorce
- Redundancy
- Retirement
- Adolescence

Quite often these events can mark the beginning of a growth process but this is not always the case.

How many people do you know that get married but continue to live their lives in exactly the same way as before?

How many people do you know who never 'get over' the death of a loved one?

How many people are made redundant but continue to live and breathe their old life and can't move on?

How many people have babies and continue to live the life of the career girl?

How many workaholics drop down dead after they retire?

The truth is no amount of external change can bring about changes on the inside – that's growth. It can be really frustrating. Is it for you?. You really want to change and you try so hard but you still end up in the same position - exactly as you were before.

I can pinpoint the moments in my life that journey took sharp turns. The first came through my difficulties to the realisation that I was going to find out what was happening to me and why.

The second was the realisation at the Sacre Coeur, in Paris that my marriage was over. It is worth noting that this thought came out of no-where and through no suffering. Although, it was about to cause a great deal of suffering.

I also can pinpoint another two events that caused my life to take a dramatic change in direction. When my heart was broken for the first time at age 29, I felt like I had been hit by a bus. The other was the night I made the decision to change my career direction.

The reason that I'm explaining this is important. It is important to understand that change/growth is either triggered by difficulty or the realisation the change will cause difficulty.

For many the triggers will come spontaneously through a thought or realisation.
William Bridges, Transition Expert, calls this a period of disenchantment. It is the realisation that things are not as they once were. You experience an increase in consciousness – a higher level of awareness. You can see things much clearer. If it is the first time you have been through a growth process, it can be frightening!

You realise the potential pain that may be caused as a consequence of this new awareness. This is why you may have avoided growth all together. Ask yourself this. Are you afraid of changing and the potential growth opportunity? Napoleon Hill who personally studied 500 of the world's most successful men (including Andrew Carnegie, Henry Ford, Thomas Edison, Alexander Graham Bell) and spent a great deal of time with them, writes extensively about the benefits that adversity can bring. Many of the best ideas and inspiration come through difficult times.

What helps at this stage?
- Be honest with yourself (next we will look at the challenges that can occur when you don't do this!)
- Find someone else you can be honest with (even if you have to pay for it). Someone who will accept you and your truth. We all need the support of others. Extreme dependence or extreme independence works for no one.
- Focus on the here and now – stop worrying about what's going to happen or what you are going to do. There is plenty of time for that.

If you came to see me at this stage I would tell you that I am excited for you. You see, I know that if you can get through the next two stages, good things are coming your way.☺

> *"All the adversity I've had in my life, all my troubles and obstacles have strengthened me... You may not realize it when it happens, but a kick in the teeth may be the best thing in the world for you."*
> **Walt Disney**

Stage 2: Resistance

Why Do You Resist?

Change and growth involve some suffering. You may not have been taught at a young age that struggle can be a perfectly natural part of growth. You may not have been taught that this is normal and that it's ok to feel hurt some of the time.

What messages did you receive when you were younger? "Don't get upset.", "Boys don't cry.", "It's wrong or weak to show emotions!" Are these familiar?

Which of these beliefs do you own? The end result is, you only fear hurt, sadness and pain. You fear and resist a perfectly natural process.

> *"What you resist persists"*
> **Carl Jung**

Your thoughts and feelings are communicating to you all the time. When you need to change something, these thoughts and feelings can become more intense.

Carl Rogers, one of the most influential psychologists who founded the humanistic approach describes this as the self actualising tendency. The actualising tendency is a persons ability to incorporate their experiences into their concept of themselves. Kids that are fortunate to be brought up in genuinely loving environments will learn to trust their thoughts and feelings and make decisions accordingly. These kids will change and grow feeling good about making decisions as they develop and experience life. For those kids who are not raised in loving environments their self concept will be based on the values of others – particularly with parents as they desire a greater need for love and approval. In order to feel safe and not be scolded, a self concept is created. The self concept can become quite rigid. Experiences that do not fit with this can be rejected or dismissed.

When experiences are not accepted a person will experience uncomfortable thoughts and feelings. These thoughts and feelings are a sign that something needs attention – something needs to change.

How You Resist
Here are some key emotions and activities that are commonly used to avoid uncomfortable thoughts and feelings.

Anger, blame and resentment – all hostile and negative emotions hold you back and not the person that you feel hostility towards. Often the people you resent are not even aware of how you feel. When you feel this way towards others you lose your self control and individual power. You take on the 'poor me' victim mentality which might make you feel better in the short term. However, you will not find longer term health and happiness by shifting the responsibility of your life onto others. You are responsible for your own life and happiness.

Fixing other people – it might be more tempting to fix other people than fix things in our own life. You might easily be able to see the fault in others rather than in yourself. But beware, this is resistance at work. Other people are just fine and will work on themselves if and when they are ready to do so. If someone asks for your help, then fine, give it. If not keep your mouth zipped and focus on yourself. People who feel good with themselves are too busy concentrating on their own lives to interfere with others. If you find yourself doing this, it should act as a neon light warning you to hold up the mirror.

Overindulgence in food, drink or drugs – think about it like this. People who are more aware/conscious /evolved (and happier) do what it takes to make themselves lighter so that they are more sensitive to their own thoughts and feelings. When you over eat or indulge more than you should with alcohol and drugs, you become heavier and are less sensitive to these inner signals. When these inner signals become too much to handle, you will deliberately block your feelings with excessive food drink or drugs. It could easily become an addiction.

Diversion/distraction – if you keep your mind busy enough you don't have to deal with your thoughts and feelings. It is the ultimate denial technique. You don't stop long enough to listen to yourself. The picture comes to mind when you were a child and you put your fingers in your ears and say "I am not listening, la la la". You may have various ways of keeping your mind busy, you may undertake a new project or projects, socialise excessively so you don't need to be alone with yourself, plan holidays or you may spend your life on Facebook watching how others are living their lives. All of these can be ways of diverting your mind from yourself.

The advice given to many is that anti-depressant medication will help to cure the conditions of mental illness. This advice is based on the belief that emotional distress is a biological/chemical imbalance. In all the years that the public has been told this theory it has **never** been proven.

The fact is, anti-depressants numb your feelings. Many, many people take anti-depressants through lack of knowledge and understanding of alternatives that are available. And many, many people become dependent longer-term on anti-depressant medication, believing they are needed to cope with daily life.

Unfortunately these people become stuck in the middle of a growth process through fear of their feelings, fear of going mad, lack of support, lack of knowledge and many other factors that CAN be changed.

What Are You Resisting?

Steven Pressfield identifies the following as the greatest hits of resistance in his book *War of Art*.

1) The pursuit of any calling in writing, painting, music, film, dance or any

creative art, however marginal or unconventional.
2) The launching of any entrepreneurial venture or enterprise, for profit or otherwise.
3) Any diet or health regimen.
4) Any program of spiritual advancement.
5) Any activity whose aim is tighter abdominals.
6) Any course or program designed to overcome an unwholesome habit or addiction.
7) Education of every kind.
8) Any act of political, moral, or ethical courage, including the decision to change for the better some unworthy pattern of thought or conduct in ourselves.
9) The undertaking of any enterprise or endeavour whose aim is to help others.
10) Any act that entails commitment of the heart. The decision to get married, to have a child, to weather a rocky patch in a relationship.
11) The taking of any principled stand in the face of adversity.

Quite frankly, he lists anything that is going to be good for you! What's more, it appears to be anything that you may have to work for and delay gratification.

Anxiety and Depression
If we resist for long enough, we will likely suffer from extreme distress, manifesting as anxiety and depression. In his book, *Beyond Prozac*, Dr. Terry Lynch details the brain imaging techniques which are currently being used in Psychiatry. Studies have proved that the area of the brain that is activated in people suffering from depression and anxiety, is the amygdala. The amygdala is the area of the brain associated with fear. Dr. Lynch states, "These results should not surprise us, since fear is a virtually ever present feature in people experiencing any form of emotional and psychological distress."

Labelling
Often, people who are severely distressed are labelled as having a 'mental illness' or as being 'mentally ill'. These labels imply that there is something abnormal or inappropriate about their experiences.

The fact is, any therapist, counsellor or alternative health practitioner will quickly tell you - there is always a reason for stress. Excess fear, stress and distress will lead to physical and mental symptoms of anxiety and depression. It is a perfectly natural response from a body put under undue pressure. There is nothing unnatural about it.

Dr. Lynch explains that, "The stigma of 'mental illness' will continue as long as the experiences of the people diagnosed as 'mentally ill' remain stigmatised. As long as society views depression, severe anxiety, so-called hallucinations and delusions, paranoia, easting distress issues, suicidal tendencies and manic behaviour as bad, wrong, incomprehensible, weird, crazy – the stigma will continue. The tragedy is that society's interpretation of these experiences is misguided."

Psychiatrist and author of *Toxic Psychiatry*, Dr. Peter Breggin outlines that the general belief amongst psychiatrists is that schizophrenia is physical brain disease. This belief is held despite there being no evidence supporting it. Breggin writes, "The early warning signs of schizophrenia strongly point not to a physical problem; they clearly suggest that the central issue in schizophrenia is a major emotional crisis characterised by **intense fear and emotional distress** rather than a physical brain disease: early warning signs include social withdrawal, isolation, reclusiveness, suspiciousness of others, deterioration and abandonment of personal hygiene, flat emotions, inability to express joy, inability to cry or excessive crying, inappropriate laughter, excessive fatigue and sleepiness or an inability to sleep."

The point is, never allow yourself to be labelled as 'mentally ill'.

You experience what you experience. It will have meaning for you even if you are not currently aware of what that is. The symptoms of severe stress, anxiety and depression can be very scary. You might feel like you are going mad or that you are mentally ill. It is fear that keeps you locked in the destructive cycles. It is fear that continues to stimulate the amygdala part of your brain.

It can be tempting when severely distressed to accept the 'mental illness' term and biological theories. We want someone to acknowledge our experience. When we accept that we are not responsible for our condition, we may receive sympathy and understanding from those around us. There is, however, a major drawback to this.

If you do not take responsibility (responsibility not blame) for your life, you lose your power. You become more vulnerable, powerless, form more dependencies and your feelings of hopelessness increase. Think about it! If you accept this theory, then there is no way of knowing if and when this 'illness' may return. The result is you live your life in fear, the very thing that created what you are currently experiencing.

This is what creates, continuous and repeated self destructive cycles. It is time to break it once and for all.

> *"Once you label me, you negate me"*
> Soren Kierkegaard

Stage 3: Letting Go

Letting go is the hardest of all the stages. It's easier to drown your sorrows or to drive yourself to distraction. Regardless of how difficult this stage is, do not underestimate it. This is the part of the process where you learn the most. This is where your understanding and lessons come from.

Letting go involves facing yourself and all the emotions that go along with it. You might swing from letting go back to resistance when the emotions get challenging. You might convince yourself that you are wrong and that others are right. You have to be brave when you are in the process of letting go.

What you might experience
- **Sadness** – when you let go you can feel great sadness. There can be a sense of loss even if someone has not died. Essentially, you need to go through a grieving process before you are ready to move forward. Many people are uncomfortable with sadness and therefore try to bypass this stage to get to a new beginning. If you bypass this stage and force a new

beginning prematurely then you miss out on the growth opportunity and the hard work will be for nothing.

- **Despair** - sadness might not be close to describing how you are feeling. Utter despair might be closer to the reality of your feelings. Again despair is not to be feared. Remember if you resist the feelings they are likely to last longer. Better to feel extreme despair for a few days, express the emotions and then move through the process. If you don't do this, the uncomfortable thoughts and feelings may linger for months and even years. There is no need for this. As I have explained some great insights/inspiration can come from moments of despair.
- **Fear** – change can be scary! It's human nature to want a sense of predictability to feel secure. When events change rapidly you can feel insecure and unsafe. You may question your ability to handle the unknown and again you may fluctuate between letting go and resistance. Fear can manifest in people in many different ways but the most common way is in

anger. This is the natural way to express fear for many people.

- **Nothingness/emptiness** – William Bridges explains this as the neutral zone. It's a period of time when the "old" way of doing things has not yet been replaced with the "new beginning". Again, this can be an uncomfortable feeling for many. Life is so busy now – iphones, internet, Facebook, twitter – we never take the time to stand still. Yet, much can be said in silence! Nothingness requires patience and acceptance of what is. It is through this silence that the inner changes will be felt. There will be an inner signal that a new beginning is on its way.
- **Frustration** – there is nothing more frustrating sitting in a period of unknown. You may be the type of person who wants everything to be planned out. Having a plan is important if you ever want to get anywhere. However, when life doesn't work out according to the plan it can be frustrating. When you are letting go of your old and limiting thoughts, beliefs and

behaviours, you don't know what the new 'you' is going to look and feel like.

Patience and acceptance

This list is not exhaustive. Again I am going to stress the importance of patience and acceptance throughout this stage more than at any other point in the process.

"Our sorrows and wounds are healed only when we touch them with compassion."

Buddha

You are vulnerable during this period and you might not feel emotionally stable – especially if these emotions have been stored away for some time. You might feel overwhelmed by them. I am going to let you into a little secret. ☺ These feelings are normal during a period of inner growth. You are not ill and there is certainly nothing wrong with you. There is nothing to be ashamed or embarrassed about.

In the meantime, until that time comes because it might be a while, you are going to have to accept and be patient.

The reason that you have to accept and be patient is because genuine new beginnings will take time to happen. They do not happen overnight and you may need time to heal.

It is also wise to be cautious of the input from other people at this stage. You want to be influenced by your own thoughts and feelings not those of others.

Frankly, other people will have something to say when you are in this stage of the process.

Generally, most people are uncomfortable with honest expressions of emotion. It makes them feel uncomfortable and they might think that there is something wrong with you.

Also you might not know where you are going next and it might look to others that you need advice about what to do or where to go next.

Don't make the mistake of not accepting genuine offers of help or encouragement. However be discriminate in your choice with whom and when you seek this support.

What can help?
- Get comfortable with spending time alone in quietness.
- Be kind to yourself mentally and physically – see the suggestions in the following sections. Make your health your number one priority – over and above anything else in your life.
- Read about persistence and learn about how to continue in the face of adversity.
- Surround yourself with people and activities that make you feel good about yourself – not as a distraction but in terms of showing yourself some compassion.

"Tell your heart that the fear of suffering is worse than the suffering itself"
Paulo Coelho

Stage 4: New Beginnings

The new beginning is the last part of the process – save the best till last some may say! Others prefer the lessons and learning that comes from the letting go stage. The reward of going through this process is the new beginnings that take place once you have let go of the old ideas/beliefs and behaviours.

A genuine new beginning will be felt from the inside. It will not be a forced external beginning i.e. a new job, marriage or house move.

A new beginning will feel refreshing, hold new perspectives, beliefs and thoughts and produce new behaviours. The early stages of a new beginning may be subtle and not obvious to those around you.

A new beginning can feel exciting as you anticipate the external change that it may bring. The "old" way of being and the "old" beliefs are a thing of the past. The new experiences have been accepted into the self concept. If you get this far you have successfully self actualised.

New beginnings are an inner process. The icing on the cake may be they bring about positive external changes in your life. The difference is the opportunities will come naturally and will feel right.

The more familiar that you become with this process, the easier it becomes to navigate yourself through these times. The less you fear and resist this natural process, the more flexible and nimble that you become.

It is unlikely once you have been through this process once that it will be the last time. The beauty of this is you learn to adapt and embrace change and growth in your life. You will be in the flow.

"There are two mistakes one can make along the road to truth… not going all the way and not starting".
Buddha

Severe Stress Symptoms

Make a list of all the symptoms that you have been experiencing.

Physical (physical sensations, ailments, aches, pains)

Mental (thoughts, thought processes)

Emotional (feelings)

In no particular order here is a list of some of the physical, mental and emotional symptoms that can be experienced when suffering from extreme stress, anxiety and depression. A high proportion of people experience anxiety and depression at the same time.

Physical symptoms
- Unexplained aches and pains
- Insomnia/disturbed sleep
- Lack of energy/fatigue
- Hyperactivity/excess energy
- Weight loss/gain
- Lack of appetite
- Loss of sex drive
- Sweating

- Difficulty breathing/shortness of breath
- Feeling sick
- Persistent muscle tension, stiffness
- Shaking/trembling
- Irregular heartbeat, flutters, palpitations
- Abdominal stress

Mental Symptoms
- Anxious/worried thoughts
- Racing thoughts, rapid or repetitive thinking
- Suicidal thoughts
- Disturbing and repulsive thoughts often of a violent/sexual nature inc. self harming
- Unable to concentrate
- Difficulty making a decision
- Fears of dying, impending doom, going crazy

Emotional
- Feeling down/low
- Feelings of unreality
- Hopelessness
- Helplessness
- Lack of enjoyment in life
- Lack of motivation

- Lack of feeling
- Over emotional/tearful
- Feeling guilty
- Low self confidence and self esteem
- Feeling angry/lack of patience

Panic Attacks

For many this can be the first symptom to occur. The first panic attack normally comes hard and fast and knocks you off your feet. You will likely:

- Feel light headed, almost like you are going to pass out.
- Feel your vision affected, like you are going to faint.
- Feel your heart racing and possibly experience chest pains (this is why many people go straight to hospital when they are experiencing their first few panic attacks)
- Feel a sense of doom, like something bad is going to happen or that you are going to die
- Have irrational thoughts and be unable to control them.

Panic attacks, whilst irrational, are the most frightening experience ever!

The only person who can truly understand the level of fear that you feel is someone that has been through the same thing. This is why it is so difficult for other people close to you to understand. It can be hugely frustrating for you and for those you love.

You may have been experiencing panic attacks for some time and therefore you may have avoided certain situations or events to prevent another attack from happening. This is common. You may have had an attack at the shops, when you are out with friends or at work. Then you avoid the place where you had the panic attack because you WRONGLY believe it is the situation or event that caused this to happen in the first place.

Let's look at why you have these symptoms and sensations and begin to understand what has been happening in your body.
Here are some tools and techniques that you can use to undo this learned behaviour quickly and effectively.

Recovery

One of the first steps in recovering from severe stress symptoms is an understanding and acceptance of what is happening to you.

Often you do not realise that extreme stress and distress affects you on a physical, mental and emotional level. Your body is highly sophisticated and communicates to you in different ways. You are often unaware that many of the physical, mental and emotional symptoms are a result of excess stress.

Your recovery may be a unique process but the symptoms that you experience are similar to anyone else who is suffering from extreme stress, anxiety or depression. You are not crazy and certainly not going mad.

As discussed, there is a stigma surrounding extreme emotional suffering which is why the majority of people suffer in silence. The increasing figures of 'mental illnesses and those on anti-depressants clearly indicate that you are not alone.

How stress affects your behaviour

I am going to briefly explain the impact this can have on the way you behave and act.

Researching your condition

You become totally consumed with researching your physical complaints. The internet serves as a breeding ground for this type of behaviour. You will likely search for the meaning and attempt to diagnose the various symptoms that you have. You will not be content with what you find, so you continue to search. The reason is because a restless mind will never stop. You will constantly be analysing and worrying over the slightest thing.

Talking about how you feel

When you are highly aware of every thought, sensation and physical symptom that you feel, you often feel the need to share these feelings with those who are closest to you. You think that you cannot cope with the sensations on your own. The trouble is that those who are close don't really get it, and can't relate to your irrational thoughts and feelings. Some of your closest family and friends can even be uncomfortable when you try to explain what is happening. This, rather than alleviate the symptoms, can make matters worse.

Avoiding certain people or activities
High levels of stress, anxiety or depression triggers your avoiding going out socially, especially places where there are lots of people. Perhaps you have stopped going to work or you have taken time off. Some people will avoid driving if this where they feel worse, and some will avoid flying and going on holidays.

As I explained early on, extreme stress affects you differently from others. It will be a physical and mental experience unique to you.

As you adapt certain things in your life to deal with your fears, they have a habit of following you. Soon you have stopped doing most or all of things that you once used to love. Even if you are normally an out-going and confident person, you can end up feeling like you are weak and worthless.

Visiting many different medical professionals
At first you may visit the Doctor's or hospital fearing for your life! Then depending on what Doctor you see you may be prescribed one of many different medications including, anti-depressants, sleeping pills, beta blockers, tranquilisers. I have been prescribed all of these medications at different times when I experienced stress and anxiety. The trouble is not one of them cured me, so I felt the need to visit different Doctors and look for yet another opinion and solution.

I wish that in the future there was no need for medication to help manage the symptoms of stress, anxiety and depression. However, I appreciate that in the current state of affairs there is still a place for it. As I was saying earlier, we tend to leave things until they are so bad that we have little alternative but to take something to alleviate the symptoms. Medication can help in the short-term whist you learn the tools and techniques described in this book. Medication is not the longer-term solution and will keep you from growing and evolving.

There are many different opinions, even within the medical profession. This is why it can be confusing if you see different doctors. The fact is doctors are trained to diagnose and prescribe medication. You want your doctor to help solve your social, psychological and emotional challenges. They may not be able to help you except prescribe medication.

To recover fully, you can listen to the advice but you must learn to listen to yourself above anyone else. This is when you will be truly free. You have to heal from the inside out. You know yourself better than any other person. You will know what is working for you and what is not. There is never only one way. The right teacher will come your way as soon as you are ready or as soon as you make the decision that you are willing to learn ☺. That's why you're reading this now.

"Know or listen to those who know."
Baltasar Gracian

Words and Actions

Your thoughts cause you to speak and act. If you want to remove stress, anxiety and depression from your life and stop creating the misery that you are experiencing, you need to look closely at the way you talk and behave.

Not only can you work on healing your mind, you can also work on the way you speak and behave. If you think about popular behaviour approaches to therapy now, you can see that these therapists effectively reverse the process. You need to understand the power of your mind and train it effectively to be free from **FEAR.**

Working on the way you speak and act only enhances the speed and effectiveness of a recovery programme.

Your Words
First you must identify what you tell yourself when you are highly stressed and anxious. Become aware what you tell others about the sensations that you are feeling and explaining just how bad it is.

You are creating what you are experiencing through your thoughts, words and actions. Therefore, you may want to think twice about what you say. You already know that it does not make the feelings or sensations any better, so what is the point in telling others about them.

Does this mean you never talk about how you feel? This is absolutely not what I am saying. No question. I will explain the importance of expressing emotions so that they do not manifest as illness and disease. I am going to provide tips for you to learn how to express yourself better emotionally. However, expressing emotions, thoughts and feelings does not mean that you need to tell others about the details of your <u>stress and anxiety symptoms</u>.

Talking about the symptoms, gives them power and attracts and perpetuates the situation. You want to reduce and eliminate these symptoms as soon as you possibly can. You want to free yourself from the misery they are creating, and you already know there is no benefit in talking about them. You want to create new experiences and new memories so that you use them to replace the horrible anxious/depressive memories.

When you stop leaning on people you will grow in strength mentally, emotionally and physically. You will build your self confidence and self esteem.

Your Actions
Now you know that the actions of **researching your condition, visiting medical professionals and avoiding certain activities or situations** only perpetuate your stress levels. Perhaps there are other ways that you could change your behaviour.

As with thoughts and words, actions are hugely important. Some professionals successfully work on adapting behaviour as a form of therapy.

Using these next mindfulness techniques, you will learn to train your mind when you are first going back to do things that you haven't done in a while. Again your confidence and self belief will increase the more that you do it.

With more practice, it will get easier.

"If you want to conquer fear, don't sit home and think about it. Go out and get busy".
Dale Carnegie

Make a list of all the ways that you have changed your behaviour

How You Create Your Experience

All the world's great leaders know that thoughts are things.

It's not just those who are interested in metaphysics and new age thought. The world's most successful people – inventors, business people, top sales professionals, religious leaders, sports professionals, political leaders, artists, writers – all utilise the power of the mind whether they are aware of it or not.

This story is a perfect illustration of this concept:

The Hall of One Thousand Mirrors

Somewhere, in a land far away, there was a temple that housed a hall of one thousand mirrors. One day it so happened that a dog got lost in the temple and arrived at this hall. Suddenly confronted with one thousand of his mirror images, he growled and barked at these presumed enemies. These, however, returned his growling and teeth flashing a thousand times over. The dog in turn got even more aggressive. And as the situation got more and more heated, the dog got more and more out of control, and finally reached such an extreme state of aggression and exertion that he dropped dead.

Some time passed, and along came another dog. He too got lost in the temple and arrived at the same hall of one thousand mirrors. This dog saw that he was surrounded by one thousand dogs of his kind. He then started to wag his tail with joy at these other dogs and, in return, one thousand dogs happily wagged their tails back at him. Happy and encouraged, the dog found a way out of the temple.

Life is mirror of our thoughts. Which way are you living?

The thoughts and emotions create the urge to speak or act. You basically attract situations, events or people to you that reflect your thoughts and emotions.

Thoughts ➡ Emotions ➡ Speak/Act

"The Greatest discovery of my generation is that human beings can alter their lives by altering their attitudes of mind."

William James

Autosuggestion and the Placebo effect

Autosuggestion was a psychological technique developed by Emile Coue, a pharmacist in the early 1900's. He would tell some patients that the drugs they were taking were known to be extremely effective. He concluded that the patients that were given positive information about certain drugs reported a higher effectiveness rate than those that received no information about the drug. This later became known as the placebo effect. This led Emile Coue into the areas of hypnotherapy and imagination.

Basically, your thoughts and beliefs about something will effect what you experience in life. This is not to say that medications do not provide therapeutic effects. The extent to which the effect is felt will depend on your beliefs about it. This is merely a recognisable and measurable example of the power of the mind.

In drug trials (randomised control trials) the effectiveness of drugs are tested against the placebo. A group is given a sugar pill – sometimes with therapeutic effects so the participants are none the wiser. The vast majority of anti-depressant drug trials do not prove that the medication is any more efficient that the placebo. In his book *Anatomy of an Epidemic*, Robert Whittaker explains that drug companies have got smarter when they are carrying out RCT's. He talks extensively about Prozac which is the only SSRI to be approved by the FDA for use with children in the United States.

Robert Whittaker explains, "There is no reason to think that Prozac is any better than the other SSRI's. The percentage of children who responded to Prozac in the two positive trials was similar to the drug response rate in the twelve failed trials; Eli Lilly simply had been better at using biased trial designs to make it *appear* that its drug worked."

For example, in one of the two Prozac trials, all of the children were initially put on placebo for one week, and if they got better during that period they were excluded from the study. This helped knock down the placebo response rate. Next, the children who were randomised onto Prozac were evaluated for a week, and only those 'who adapted well' to the drug were enrolled in the study.

What this proves is that drugs are no more effective than placebo (autosuggestion and imagination). This is a very powerful fact indeed. Rather than convince people they need to take a pill to trick their mind, why not teach people how to use their mind effectively.

Autosuggestion and the use of creative imagination are the foundations for what you create in your life - through your thoughts and mental picturing. You may have experienced success or failure in certain areas of your life. Whether you have been aware of it or not, you are using these techniques.

Napoleon Hill's, *Think and Grow Rich* and Maxwell Maltz's, *Psych-cybernetics* books have stood the test of time because what they teach works. Changing your thoughts and mental picturing through continuous and repetitive action and practice WILL re-programme your subconscious mind. Thomas Edison, Theodore Roosevelt, E.M. Statler, Alexander Graham Bell, Vince Lombardi, Dan Kennedy, Tom Butler Bowden all testified to the techniques described by these men. These people have mastered the use of their imagination for creating positive experiences.

Can you imagine that you are able to use these techniques to create success, healthy and happiness?

If the answer is yes, you need to accept that thoughts not only influence your behaviour and your experience but also that thoughts affect the body.

This might be hard for your logical/analytical brain to accept. It will probably go against everything that you have ever been taught about health/illness/disease. Likely, you were socially conditioned to believe that you are not responsible for your health – that there is no explanation for the many ailments that you suffer.

What I want to impart to you is that you are creating ALL of your physical experience. Your mind creates what happens in your body. I have listened to those who know. This is particularly the case when you are suffering from extreme stress and distress. The body can become a great communication tool.

Think of this as an example:

You are watching a very scary movie and your mind goes into overdrive – your mind starts to think some scary thoughts like 'what if there is someone outside' or 'imagine that happened to me'. Your mind might even play out a scary movie (imagining it was happening to you). All of these thoughts lead to a great sense of fear and this might affect your behaviour. You might turn the film off or turn all the lights on.

But what happens to you physically? This great sense of fear and doom consumes you. You might experience an increase in heart rate, sweaty hands, tapping your feet, or dry mouth.

When you live in a state of high stress, either mentally or physically, your body starts to perceive everyday activities as 'dangerous' and produces more adrenalin. Your body believes that this is the normal level of adrenalin. You will then have the fight or flight responses as you go about everyday activities at work, out shopping, or driving.

Your behaviour adapts because you have these extreme feelings of fear when you are doing normal things.

You are aware that this is irrational and illogical so you start to research and analyse to find out what the cause is. This can lead to a quick downward spiral from which you can find it difficult to break free.

When the body has been under **PROLONGED STRESS** the messages are sent to the brain that this increased adrenalin is normal. In order to stop experiencing the symptoms you must therefore stop the messages being sent to the brain that the increased adrenalin level is the norm.

To stop the high stress symptoms you need to reduce the level of adrenalin in your system. There is one thing stopping you from doing that and that is **FEAR** and I am going to teach you how to remove this fear. When you remove the fear of what you are experiencing your adrenalin levels will return to a normal level. This is when your symptoms will stop.

You see what has happened to your body is a normal reaction to increased adrenalin levels. It is perfectly natural and your body is working normally to increased stress. There is nothing unnatural about it. It does not mean that you are unwell or that you are mad or mentally ill. There is a perfectly reasonable explanation as to why you feel like you do.

Every day, mostly unconsciously, you think thousands of thoughts. Every day these thoughts affect your speech and behaviour. Every day these thoughts create emotions. These emotions can be felt in your human body – they are often stored there and manifest out as discomfort.

If emotions are stored there for a pro-longed period, this creates dis-ease in the body. This concept might be a little difficult to grasp initially but once we understand it, the concept can be incredibly liberating.

You see, you are not a powerless physical being with little control over what happens to you. There is not some unexplainable reason or biological defect as to why you experience any physical discomfort. You are in fact a powerful being with the ability to create illness, but you also have great healing power, to heal yourself and prevent future illness and disease.

The story of Norman Cousins highlights this. He was the Editor in Chief of the *Saturday Review* in the United States for 35 years. He spent much of his time as an advocate for world peace of which seen the invitation to meet Albert Einstein (his proudest moment). He later devoted much of his time writing about the issues of illness and healing.

Norman Cousins was plagued with illness through-out his life. He was diagnosed with tuberculosis when he was eleven years old and he was sent to hospital for the long-term sick. In the 1960's he was diagnosed as having a form of arthritis that affects the back and other joints. He was given a 1 in 500 chance of survival!

Faced with death he took matters into his own hands. He took responsibility for his recovery with the support of his Doctor friend. He researched his condition and found that the medication he was on was depleting his body of Vitamin C. He asked to be taken off of these medications and given large injections of Vitamin C.

He also checked himself out of hospital, feeling it was no place for someone unwell to be and checked himself into a hotel. Here he purchased several funny films including the Marx Brothers movies. He found he was able to stimulate chemicals through laughter that gave him pain relief.

Basically, he laughed himself back to health and within a few weeks was back to work at the *Saturday Review*.

It has been questioned whether this is the placebo effect at work again. Norman Cousins used his creative imagination to induce feelings of wellness and health and his body responded appropriately – reducing pain until he was well again.

He also held the position of Adjunct Professor of Medical Humanities for the School of Medicine at the University of California. Here he did research on the biochemistry of human emotions. He believed that emotions are the key to human beings success in fighting illness.

Normal Cousins survived:
- 10 years after his first heart attack
- 26 years after his collagen illness
- 36 years after his doctors first diagnosed his heart disease

He died in 1990 but his work continues on in the Cousins Centre for Psychoneuroimmunology. It is an interdisciplinary organisation which investigates the connection between the brain and body, the importance of mental health for recovery and provision of behavioural techniques to prevent illness and enable wellness.

Remember there would be more research into these techniques if there was any money to be made in it. In fact, people taking responsibility for their health has the opposite effects and actually threatens many professions.

> *"It is reasonable to expect the doctor to recognize that science may not have all the answers to problems of health and healing."*

Norman Cousins

Whilst not the mainstream, there are scientists out there that support this theory. Neuroscientist, Dr. Candice Pert's life work has led her to the conclusion that the mind/body is connected and gives full details in her book, *Molecules of Emotion*. The book clarifies that the immune system, endocrine system, nervous system, brain (all the main systems of the body) are in communication with each other through neuropeptides and their receptors, thus linking brain, body and behaviour.

Dr. Candice Pert concludes that the neuropeptides are molecules of emotion. They are produced primarily in the brain and are the brain chemicals of mood and behaviour which communicate with all of the bodily systems. This in turn creates the emotion that influences our physiological response, our physical reality.

"I ADMIT THOUGHTS INFLUENCE THE BODY"

ALBERT EINSTEIN

It highlights the importance of viewing the body as a whole and not separate. Just like Norman Cousins, Dr. Pert clearly explains that the real progressions in science have been made when the 'separate' areas of science began to work together in cohesion with each other (immunologists, pharmacologists, endocrinologists, neuroscientists).

Dr. Pert explains that there are nodal points in our body that are dense with neuropeptides. The nodal points run down the centre of your body as does your endocrine system and your nerve plexus. Interestingly these nodal points identified fit perfectly with the chakra/meridian energy system - an eastern philosophy which is used in most alternative health practices.

"Our body is really the product of our thoughts. We're beginning to understand in medical science the degree to which the nature of thoughts and emotions actually determines the physical substance and structure and function of our bodies".

Dr John Hagelin

2
Train Your Mind

This will help you to:
1. Develop awareness of your thoughts
2. Identify negative thought patterns
3. Explore techniques to gain better mind control

In order to achieve lasting peace of mind you will need to explore the underlying causes of your severe stress and distress. You need to be willing to examine your beliefs, how these were formed and become prepared to let go of all your emotional baggage.

The techniques described previously of autosuggestion and creative imagination will have limited value if you are holding on to old negative beliefs about yourself and the world.

This process is often best supported through counselling, therapy, coaching or mentoring. Further sources of help are identified and listed at the end of this guide.

The following mindfulness techniques can be used effectively to reduce and remove the symptoms that you are currently experiencing.

1) Becoming Aware of Your Thoughts

Why? Remember every thought you think is creating your future;

Thoughts ➡ Emotions ➡ Speak/Act

The first step is to become aware of what your thoughts are. At the moment you may be completely unconscious as what you think about all day long. Repetitive thoughts become beliefs. Beliefs become deeply engrained in our subconscious mind. If you want to use your creative imagination to build a better life, you must be aware of what these thoughts are.

Think back to the past when you have been at a crucial moment in your life – a job interview, speaking publically or teeing off on the golf course. The thoughts that you have can make or break the situation. Often you are not aware of them. You identify with them. You believe them to be true.

Note
- You are not your thoughts.
- Rather than feel frustrated at your thoughts, take responsibility!
- Welcome the opportunity to start making changes in your life. It can be fun!
- Do the following exercise to help you become more aware of your thoughts and to regain better mind control.

Exercise
This exercise is called watch the thinker extracted from the book, *The Power of Now*, by Eckhart Tolle. I recommend that you read this book when you can. You need to become the watcher of your thoughts as often as you can. Start to chase them.

If you are able to watch/observe your thoughts, then the essence of you is something else. You are something much bigger. You want to be able to stop identifying with the thoughts you have. Try it now. Start to become aware of your thoughts. Sit in a quiet place and see how long you can quieten your mind before it runs off. This time, however, I want you to catch yourself and see where your thoughts going. What are you thinking about?

At the moment your thoughts are perhaps racing, scary or irrational. You will feel like you have little control over them.

This is the important part. If you learn to watch and become the observer of your thoughts you realise that essence of you is something greater. If you can watch your thoughts, there is something else. The mind, body and spirit are all connected.

But you are NOT your thoughts. Your mind may have become lazy and you are letting your thoughts control you. You need to learn to take better control of your mind. You can learn to think and use your imagination when you need to and more effectively.

Thoughts are only thoughts that come and go. <u>When you become aware of your thoughts and can accept them without resisting, you will move from being in your head to your body.</u> This takes you out of your mind (which if not being used constructively, only replays the past or anticipates the future) into the present moment. When you enter the present moment, become focused on your sensations, what you see, hear, smell, taste, touch and feel. In the present moment (the now) you can step by step change your life.

Do this as often as you can and make a note of positive and negative thinking. You want to keep and enhance positive thinking and eliminate negative thinking. The movie *The Peaceful Warrior* might help you to understand this further.

Notes Page

How did you get on?

Your Comments

Signature _____   Date _____

Action Points

Signature _____   Date _____

"The primary cause of unhappiness is never the situation but the thought about it. Be aware of the thoughts you are thinking. Separate them from the situation, which is always neutral. It is as it is."

Echart Tolle

2) Identify Negative Thoughts

Write a list of all the negative, anxious or depressing thoughts that you are having. You might find yourself thinking, I can't sleep, or I can't relax. You need to become aware of the thoughts that you are having because as I explained earlier, this is what is creating your experience. For example, if you think all day long that you cannot sleep or that you are unable to get to sleep, this is what your reality will be.

You will need to change these thoughts before you will start to see an improvement. For now make a list and increase your awareness. You might not even have noticed until now what your thoughts have been.

Notes Page
_____
_____
_____
_____
_____
_____

How did you get on?

> Your Comments
>
> Signature _____ Date _____

> Action Points
>
> Signature _____ Date _____

"As a single footstep will not make a path on the earth, so a single thought will not make a pathway in the mind. To make a deep physical path, we walk again and again. To make a deep mental path, we must think over and over the kind of thoughts we wish to dominate our lives."

Henry David Thoreau

3) Letting go of Limiting Beliefs

Louise L Hay in *You Can Heal Your Life*, describes the process of letting go very simply and is a process that I refer back to frequently. When you find yourself unhappy about situations, people or events, there will be a limiting belief that is lurking about in the background.

This is what causes these circumstances to attract themselves to you. The reason that you attract these is because there is some need/belief within to have this situation, relationship, job, eating habit or whatever it may be. The outer experience is really a reflection of what is going on inside. For example, if you have stress and anxiety, it may be that you do not trust the process of life. You do not believe that you will be safe and that events will turn out for the best. Through your fears, beliefs and lack of trust you may have attracted the situation to you.

If you are feeling depressed, you may have a belief that you are not worthy to enjoy the pleasures of life.

It may be that you need help and support to identify your limiting beliefs. Please refer to Section 5 for more support.

Top Tips
- Use the following exercise to first clarify the outer experience that you are dissatisfied with
- Be prepared to accept responsibility for the inner need within you to have this experience
- Be prepared and willing to change – tell the universe
- Back-up with new affirmations

Exercise
1) Think about the outer experience that you are having. What situations/circumstances are causing you difficulty? What is not working well?
2) Then ask the question, "What need is within me to have this situation?" Take your time with the response. It may take a while to breakthrough, like peeling the layers of an onion. I tend to find that I am hitting a nerve when I feel emotional. I find that I can see quite clearly. You may feel anger or another form of resistance. Once you accept responsibility (not blame) for having this need then you are able to

start the process that will set you free. Having this increased level of self awareness and re-training the subconscious mind will allow the situation to change naturally

3) Tell yourself frequently that you are willing to change, over and over again.
4) Then make a list of all the things that you are willing to release. List each behaviour and start with "I release the need to _____."

Use the following Notes Pages to record your thoughts and observations or record on the worksheet at the end of the workbook. This worksheet formulates the whole process and you can use at any point in the future. I follow this process frequently, whenever I learn there is something else to let go!

Notes Page

How did you get on?

Your Comments

Signature _____ Date _____

Action Points

Signature _____ Date _____

"Beliefs have the power to create and the power to destroy. Human beings have the awesome ability to take any experience of their lives and create a meaning that dis-empowers them or one that can literally save their lives."
Tony Robbins

4) Forgiveness

Life is Now – you want to be able to come into the present moment and to start creating more positive experiences for yourself.

You want to learn to forgive yourself and those whom you believe have harmed you in any way. Forgiveness is the most effective yet potentially painful method of releasing you from the past.

Anger, resentment, bitterness and jealousy towards yourself or any other person will only hurt **you,** not the other person. The majority of the time, the other person may not even be aware that you feel this way.

Lack of forgiveness is one sure way of keeping you stuck in the past, unable to move forward. You may not even be aware of these feelings. They may be stored subconsciously and through memories and associations you have, affect your decisions.

Choosing to forgive someone does not mean that you need to agree with the actions that person took. You can choose to see that they were acting unconsciously. When you are able to see others for who they really are and you are able to forgive them, you are to forgive yourself. You are able to accept yourself, warts and all!

Note
- This is not a one-time process. You will need to repeat this process time and time again. Each time you find that things are not working for you, dig a little deeper.
- Use the previous exercise to first clarify what your limiting beliefs are.
- Be prepared to accept responsibility for the inner need within you to have this experience.
- Be prepared and willing to change.
- Forgiveness does not make you wrong or weak, quite the opposite. It takes strength to be able to forgive someone.
- Applying the principle of forgiveness will free you and bring more peace to your mind than anything else.
- Sometimes you are hardest on yourself. Forgiving others makes it easier to go

easier on yourself. You are human and continuously learning.
- Nothing bothers your enemies more than you forgiving them!

Exercise
1) 1. Make a list of names. To begin the process of forgiving others, write down the name of every person (even if they are no longer living) who has irritated or offended you in some way. If that hurt or upset is still with you, their name goes on the list. You will be amazed at the memories that come to you. People may come to your mind that you haven't thought about in years. Feel free to include your pets on the list if that feels appropriate to you. Also, be sure to put your own name on the list to forgive yourself for regrets that you may have. Keep writing names until you can't think of anyone else to add.
2) Detail what actions that you will forgive. For each person make a detailed list of what actions, behaviours, things that occurred that caused offence, hurt, and irritation to you.

3) Spend some time forgiving each person on your list. Look at the first name on your list. Close your eyes and then hold the image of each person in your mind and tell him or her, "I forgive you and I release you. My forgiveness for you is total. I am free and you are free." Once you say the affirmation, feel the truth of these words in your body. Feel how good it feels to let go. Continue to do this with each person on your list.
4) Notice how you feel and write about your experience. After you "speak to" the last person, pause for a moment to notice how you feel. You can write about your experience if you wish.
5) Express and feel your gratitude

Notes Page

_____
_____
_____
_____
_____
_____

How did you get on?

```
Your Comments




Signature _____  Date _____
```

```
Action Points




Signature _____  Date _____
```

"Darkness cannot drive out darkness; only light can do that. Hate cannot drive out hate; only love can do that"
Martin Luther King, Jr.

5) Visualisation and Meditation

Up to now, you are learning that you are not your thoughts. You know that your repetitive thoughts are creating your future. Now it's time to learn how to focus your mind.

There are a number of techniques that can be used to focus the mind. Visualisation and meditation are good places to start. If you want to be able to listen to your intuition, you need to learn how to quiet the mind long enough to hear that deeper, wiser voice.

Meditation can be challenging to begin with (particularly when suffering from stress, anxiety and depression) and it may be better to start with guided visualisations or something similar.

There are plenty products on the market – choose one that feels right for you.

Once you are more focused, you want to start using your mind constructively – to retrain your subconscious mind. To do this, you use the process of creative imagination/visualisation.

"WHAT THE MIND of man CAN CONCEIVE and believe, it CAN achieve"
Napoleon Hill

The reason why visualisation techniques work is because the subconscious mind does not know the difference between what is real and what is imagined. Remember the effect that watching a scary movie can have? The fears are not real yet they impact behaviour and the physical body. You create this fear through your thoughts and mental picturing (imagining).

You want to use the same process to create positive feelings and experiences. Do this through visualisation. If you can see it and feel it in your mind's eye, then you have the ability to create the experiences in real life.

Note
- Take the time to meditate or visualise on a daily basis to receive the maximum benefit.
- Get up earlier in the morning or spend some time in the evening when you have quiet time alone.

- Practice, practice, practice! It can take a while to get the hang of it but stick with it. Build your time up gradually.

Exercise
- When meditating, find a comfortable, quiet space where you can sit upright. Personally, I like to use the so-hum mantra that Deepak Chopra describes in his book, *SynchroDestiny*. First, become conscious of your breath and as you breathe in deeply, think to yourself, *sooooo*. Then on the out breath think *hum*, all the while staying focused on your breathing. When you become conscious of your thoughts, focus again on your breath until the mind becomes still. It may be that you may find this challenging to begin with so even start off doing it for 5 minutes and build up your time gradually. Make relaxation through meditation a daily activity and you will notice many positive changes in your life.
- Even if you are unsure about what it is you want, you are still able to create positive feelings and experiences. You can

use this technique to help. Think about a past memory that brings you complete Joy and Love, one of your favourite experiences and practice thinking about this periodically through-out the day for 15 seconds without interrupting! (Andy Shaw, *A Bug Free Mind*) Again, this will be tricky to begin with and your mind might only manage a few seconds but continue and you will get there. Remember every single detail – what happened, how you *felt*. The more you do this, the better you will feel. You are learning to focus and concentrate your mind.

- For those of you that are clear about what you want in your life, first write down the details. Then start to mentally picture in your mind's eye, the experience. What happens? Who do you talk to? How do you feel? Again, it is best to be as detailed as possible. The purpose of this exercise is to feel the experience – you see yourself succeeding, see yourself feeling confident, see yourself fit, laughing and enjoying yourself.

Believe in yourself, have fun and enjoy it! It needs to feel good.

Notes Page

How did you get on?

```
Your Comments




Signature _____ Date _____
```

```
Action Points




Signature _____ Date _____
```

"Whether you think you can or think you can't - you are right."
Henry Ford

6) Gratitude

You cannot feel depressed and feel grateful at the same time.

You can enhance good feelings through practicing gratitude. Learning how to be grateful for everything that happens in your life can take time if you have developed a number of negative habits.

Everything in life happens for a reason. You may have labelled them as "good" and "bad". The truth is that whatever life presents you 'is as it is' neither bad nor good. Every situation offers you the opportunity to grow and develop. If you need to learn something, you will experience the same situations over and over until you have learned the lesson.

Gratitude is not a tick box exercise. It is a perspective on life. It's about learning to see the good in situation and being genuinely thankful for life. It is the difference of flowing with life or resisting it. If you are ungrateful, you lack acceptance of 'what it is'. As I talked about before, resistance to 'what is', stunts growth and development – no one but you loses in this situation.

The most important aspect of expressing gratitude is making sure this is not another thing on your to do list. You have to think about that for which you are grateful and you have to focus on the feelings to go along with it. You have to **<u>feel</u>** grateful, feel the gratitude for all that's in your life and all that you want to attract in to your life.

It's important this becomes a part of your daily life. Not only for expressing thanks for what's in your life currently, but also for what you want to attract into your life. Remember your subconscious mind does not know the difference. If you want to manifest future desires, always refer in the present tense, like you have it now, otherwise it will always remain in the future.

Note
- Find the lesson in every situation in life, be grateful for every experience. If you find the blessing, you will be able to move forward and avoid getting "stuck".
- Remember this is not another thing to add to the 'to do' list - you have to immerse yourself in the feelings of gratitude that go along with the thoughts. It will help you

to attract many good things in to your life, whatever it is that you want.
- It is impossible to feel any negative feelings when you are in a feeling of gratitude.

Exercise
- There are a couple of ways in you can practice daily gratitude. You could make a list before you go to bed at night. This may be hard initially, therefore spend time during the day thinking about the many things you could be grateful for. As you practice it will become easier.
- Alternatively, you don't have to write them in a list format, you could do this mentally through out the day. However, I believe when you start doing this it is easier and helps you to become more disciplined to write it down. If you practice daily gratitude and then stop, you will notice a substantial change in your feelings (try it for a minimum of 30 days).
- Create 'Your Memorable Moments List'. See Appendix. This should be a list of your most memorable and favourite

experiences. Don't write the things you think you 'should'. This is private – for your benefit only, therefore, chose the memories that give you the most pleasure. Spend 15 minutes a day looking at your list (you may choose to do this rather than meditating). Remember the details, really visualise yourself there. What did it feel like? Be thankful for all the good times that you had.

Notes Page

How did you get on?

Your Comments

Signature _____ Date _____

Action Points

Signature _____ Date _____

"Every adversity, every failure, every heartache carries with it the seed on an equal or greater benefit".
Napoleon Hill

7) Affirmations

You can re-train your subconscious mind through the use of positive affirmations. Positive affirmations are basically positive statements that re-affirm what you want to be, feel or achieve.

I shared the analogy of putting icing on a mould cake. For that reason I have deliberately left affirmations to the end. Positive thinking can be helpful to succeed but the mere use of affirmations will not work. You have to go through the steps of identifying and letting go of limiting beliefs before they will work. They can be used to help alleviate the distressing symptoms of excess stress, anxiety or depression.

If you are willing to use affirmations, they can enhance re-training the subconscious mind. Like any thoughts, if you say them over and over again, you will eventually believe them to be true.

Note
- Start affirmations with I am, I have, I can (always in the present tense)
- Say your affirmation in your mind whenever you remember, through-out the day.

- Write your affirmations down on paper, daily preferably
- Write your affirmation down and put it somewhere that you can see it frequently
- Put feeling in to your affirmation, believe it to be true.
- Look in the mirror and say your affirmation to yourself.
- Example "I am a relaxed and at peace"

Exercise
- Revisit your previous notes where you recorded your negative thoughts. This may help you to identify affirmations that may be helpful for you.
- Whenever your negative, repetitive, distressing thoughts make an appearance do not resist, let them wash over you. Say to yourself STOP and replace with a positive affirmation.
- For example. If one of your negative thoughts is, I can't sleep, each time you notice that thought, relax and, say, "STOP! I have a wonderful, relaxing sleep. Thank you!"

- You can also say affirmations at a time of day that suits you or you may say them frequently in your mind through out the day. For example, say outloud, "I am calm and relaxed. All is well in my world. I am flexible and flowing with life."

"Nurture your mind with great thoughts for you will never go higher than you think"
Benjamin Disraeli

Notes Page

_____

_____

_____

_____

_____

_____

_____

_____

How did you get on?

Your Comments

Signature _____ Date _____

Action Points

Signature _____ Date _____

"You've got to win in your mind before you win in your life."
John Addison

8) Diversion

You can also use the technique of diverting your mind from anxious or depressive thought spirals. Does it work? Yes, I used it personally. However, if you do not learn the other techniques that I have outlined then you will never really learn to master your own mind. If you have to use diversion as your only technique you are effectively resisting your thoughts rather than training your mind. The FEAR will remain longer term. I want you to live free from any fear in your life.

Particularly in the height of stress/anxiety/depression, this can be a very useful technique. To divert your mind from your thoughts you can engage in an activity that requires your full focus. You can do anything that makes it difficult for you to allow your mind to wander. Watching TV does not work as you can be sitting in front of the TV and not actually watching it.

Perhaps you have an engaging interest or hobby that you can get involved with. I found the evenings a challenge when I was recovering and was restricted to the house with two young children. Although not the most exciting hobby, I found myself cross stitching in the evening to relaxing music and it was hugely beneficial. Find something that works well for you. Examples are photography, cooking, gardening, or whatever fancies you.

Notes Page

How did you get on?

Your Comments

Signature _____ Date _____

Action Points

Signature _____ Date _____

> "YOU CANNOT BE BOTH UNHAPPY AND FULLY PRESENT IN THE NOW."
> **ECKHART TOLLE**

3
Build Your Physical Strength

This will help you to:
1. Understand the importance of managing emotions.
2. Identify your stressors and ways to eliminate them.
3. Explore the various approaches to improve physical health and wellbeing.

1) Emotions

Science is now teaching what many spiritual teachers have known for years: that thoughts manifest in the physical body in the form of emotions. To appreciate the importance of managing your emotions, you have to be prepared to work on taking control of your mind and your physical body.

Up to now, you have learned that your beliefs/thoughts in life are manifesting through your emotional body as health or disease in your physical body. Your endocrine and nervous systems are the sources. Basically, that means is if you don't express what you are feeling, you are likely to experience physical discomfort, illness which could lead to disease. It is therefore really important for you to express your feelings, including your positive feelings. Suppressing love and compassion can be just as harmful as suppressing negative emotions.

It may be that through expressing your emotions that you become aware of limiting beliefs/judgements that you hold. This allows you to make a choice – to either hold on to these beliefs or let go of the ones that are no longer serving you.

Note

- Find friends who accept you as you are, and with whom you are completely comfortable and can openly express how you feel.
- Own your emotions, if you feel happy, sad, angry, frustration, admit and own your feelings. State how the

events/circumstances are making you feel but don't blame anyone else.
- If you want to find a good way to release anger, find somewhere private, close the door and punch a pillow really hard continuously until you have released all your anger. Personally, I find running helpful.
- Allow yourself to feel whatever it is you are feeling. Many try to avoid feelings of sadness but sadness is part of life. If you feel sad, embrace, wallow in it until the feeling passes. Avoiding this feeling will only allow it to linger for longer.
- If you have events from the past that are unresolved it may be worthwhile seeking support from a counsellor or psychotherapist.
- It may be worthwhile joining a group for support. However be cautious. The unconditional positive support you can receive in a group can be hugely beneficial in allowing you to express your true self. They need to be well managed. Some groups can dwell

on the past and revisit the same things over and over again.
- Don't dwell on the past for too long. Lack of forgiveness only hurts you and not the other person.
- Find ways to express yourself. Music and arts are excellent vehicles. Personally, I find writing to be hugely beneficial in expressing my thoughts and feelings.
- If anxious or depressive feelings are prolonged it is important to seek professional help.

Exercise
- If you don't already have friends/family where you can be yourself completely and openly express how you feel then make plans and find opportunities to make new friends. Ask yourself honestly, do you have depth to your relationships or are your relationships of a superficial nature?
- Identify effective outlets to express your 'negative emotions', spending time in nature, exercise, talking, expressing, crying

or whatever it may be. Find what works best for you.
- Find a counsellor/therapist if you have past issues to resolve so that you can move forward effectively. There are various techniques and approaches to therapy, so make sure you take some time, learn about the approaches and choose one that you feel will work well for you.
- Our emotions can be an effective sign of mental patterns that need to be changed. If this is the case, then spend some time on healing your mind.
- If you have an outlet to express yourself creatively, then great, continue doing this! If not, find one as soon as you can. Is there something that you are drawn to? Is there something that you have always wanted to do but keep putting off?

Notes Page

How did you get on?

Your Comments

Signature _____ Date _____

Action Points

Signature _____ Date _____

"Comfort in expressing your emotions will allow you to share the best of yourself with others, but not being able to control your emotions will reveal your worst."
Bryant H. McGill

2) Stress

In the United States stress has been called the 'health epidemic of the 21st century' by the World Health Organisation and is estimated to cost up to £300 billion dollars.

In the UK, employers report that stress accounts for 40% of all sickness absence. The current economic pressure has put so much pressure on people that stress rates are increasing at alarming number.

Continuing to live in this way puts enormous pressure on the body. As Dr. Candice Pert explains, when your body perceives danger, a part of your brain called the hypothalamus is stimulated which affects many different parts of your body. The hypothalamus is the emotional part of the brain which extends to the pituitary gland and is the main gland in the endocrine system. CRF (cortical releasing factor) hits the pituitary gland which stimulates the secretion of ACTH that travels through the blood to the adrenal glands which release adrenalin.

The adrenalin in your body prepares you for the 'fight' or 'flight' response. The increased amount of adrenalin stimulates the heart and the liver releases extra amounts of sugar into the blood stream for extra energy. The digestive system slows as the blood is re-routed to the muscles. This response in your body is a totally natural defence mechanism and protects you when you are in dangerous situations.

There are numerous occasions that are stressful and when they are short-term this should not cause any problems. However if you experience these physical changes on a longer-term basis, you can start to encounter problems.

For many, prolonged periods of stress, result in anxiety and depression. This then produces a whole host disturbing physical and mental symptoms.

Note
- Learn more about the importance of diet, exercise, sleep, bodywork, laughter.
- With already increased sugar levels in the blood, look to stabilise your blood sugar levels. Dr. Katharina Dalton treated clients in her clinics for this recommends a 3 hour

starch diet which can help to stabilise blood sugar levels.
- Breathing exercises are really important and you can use a guided visualisation CD or meditation to support you in breathing correctly. Yoga and Tai Chi also use breathing techniques as part of the teachings. Alternatively it may be worthwhile finding out more about the Alaxander Technique.
- Surround yourself with people in life who make you feel good, who support you unconditionally and want the best for you. Life is far too short for negativity, confrontation or people who drain your energy.
- Identify and face the things in life that are causing us stress, whatever that may be, finances, relationships, careers. Denial results in more stress!!!
- Find things that you love to do and that help you to relax - healthy, nourishing activities that are good for the soul.
- It is very important to take the opportunities that arise to have some time

for yourself, especially if you have a family.
- Most importantly you need to love yourself, feel fulfilled and live the life you want. This is the biggest lesson and blessing that you can give your children. To set the example to live happy.

Exercise
What are your stressors? Maybe your busy lifestyle feels natural to you whereby someone else finds being busy is stressful. For others being too quiet will cause enormous stress. It's important you get to know yourself better. Make a list of all the things that cause stress in your life no matter how minor they seem. What events stress you out? What people, activities, things cause stress in your life?

Eliminate – start to go through your list and look for ways to reduce these situations in your life. Remember you have a choice what you do with your life, who you spend time with and what your priorities are. Where can you do things differently? Get more help and support? There is always a different way of doing things. There is always a solution.

Make a decision – procrastination is the biggest effect of failing to make effective decisions. The attempt to avoid or dismiss making decisions will result in more stress in your life. Look through your list and start to make decisions that will bring positive change into your life.

Make a plan – putting plans in place will help you to get organised! Include everything from clearing out your desk and your cupboards to important life plans. Getting organised helps to focus and move forward rather than getting 'stuck' in the stressors which you created!

Notes Page

_____
_____
_____
_____
_____
_____
_____
_____
_____
_____

How did you get on?

Your Comments

Signature _____ Date _____

Action Points

Signature _____ Date _____

"Pain is a relatively objective, physical phenomenon; suffering is our psychological resistance to what happens. Events may create physical pain, but they do not in themselves create suffering. Resistance creates suffering. Stress happens when your mind resists what is... The only problem in your life is your mind's resistance to life as it unfolds."
Dan Millman

3) Diet

This is not going to be a lecture on healthy eating – that's everywhere at the moment and people are still getting fatter by the minute. Healthy eating information and advice in isolation is useless. If you over eat then there is likely an emotional reason for it.

You over eat for any one of the following reasons:
- You have a poor self image/concept
- You lack self confidence and self acceptance
- To make you feel better
- To block uncomfortable thoughts and feelings
- Resistance to change

Basically, it is an internal issue. This is the reason diets and the many other products that deal with 'weight loss', rarely work long-term. If however, you combine working with your internal issues as well as your diet, you will achieve more lasting results.

Food is fuel. Food gives you energy. Food can be enjoyed but it is not intended as an emotional band aid to make you feel better. I have already talked about the importance of addressing your limiting beliefs and expressing your emotions.

If you were to fill your car with rubbish it would not work properly and the same idea applies to our body. If you want to function properly and increase your energy levels, then you must eat and drink foods to help you achieve this. Your body needs plenty of nutrients, fresh fruit and vegetables, fibre, protein and less saturated fats that will make you feel sluggish and deplete energy levels.

My own experience has taught me that diet changes take time. It is normally a gradual process. Rome wasn't built in day and I wanted the changes to stick. I have made gradual changes to my diet over the past few years.

Where do you start? Listen to your intuition – you will likely have had repetitive thoughts and feelings about the foods and drinks that you should eliminate. Mine started with chocolate and then moved on to other things – alcohol, tea, meat. These foods would often make me feel bad after I ate them. What makes you feel bad after you eat?

The best way to stay committed, is to make a 100% commitment for yourself. If you do something only at 90/95% of the time, there will always be a battle going on inside your head. – will I/wont I. Once you commit to something (like stop eating sweets/chocolate) there is no room for that battle in your head.

Note
- Remember, everything in moderation! If you are making changes to your diet try having smaller portions or if you are trying to eliminate certain foods, let it be a gradual process. There is no need to put unnecessary pressures on yourself.
- Try to include as many fruit and vegetables in to your diet as possible.
- Make sensible choices and choose more healthy carbs and whole grains
- Fats are essential in our diet but again choose healthy fats as opposed to unhealthy fats.
- A healthy diet includes protein and calcium.
- Try to limit the amount of sugar and salt that you intake.

Exercise
- Become more conscious of what you are eating and note where you eat certain foods excessively or where you feel bad after you eat certain things.
- It you are unaware of what a healthy diet should contain, seek nutritional information and advice from the internet or health professionals.
- Take some time to plan lunches and dinners for the week ahead. If we don't plan ahead we are more likely to snack or eat fast food. Make as many home-made meals as possible and freeze portions.
- Be aware of making the assumption that certain foods are good for you. After a recent consultation with a Kinesiologist who does individual food testing, I was surprised by the results. If you are open to alternative medicine, Kinesiology is excellent. The results are unique to your own body.

Notes Page

How did you get on?

Your Comments

Signature _____ Date _____

Action Points

Signature _____ Date _____

"The doctor of the future will give no *medication*, but will interest his patients in the care of the human frame, *diet* and in the cause and prevention of disease."
Thomas A Edison

4) Exercise

You want to be able to feel what is going on in your body and to flow with life. The solution is to keep your body flexible and nimble.

Again, to sustain exercise for the longer-term, it must become a part of your daily or weekly routine. Believe it or not, you can actually come to enjoy exercise. I would never have thought this possible a few years ago.

If exercise is merely a means to an end such as losing weight, it will likely be a short term measure. Like food, regular exercise gives you energy. You should exercise to feel good.

The psychological benefits of exercise are just as important as the physical benefits. A regular exercise programme makes you feel good about yourself, gives you more confidence, and makes you feel stronger emotionally and mentally.

So start to question any limited beliefs that you may have about exercise. "I'm not sporty." , "I am too fat!" , "I can't run." , "I don't have time.", "I can't afford to." You need to challenge any of these negative voices that are quite simply not true. If you really want to change and get in shape then there is absolutely nothing stopping you but you.

There are so many options for exercise – find things that are fun. It doesn't have to break the bank. The obvious option is to join a gym and this may work for some people but personally it bores me to tears. If money is tight then it does not cost a lot to buy a decent pair of trainers and go out walking/running. Remember to start off small (round the block), and gradually build up distance.

It can take a while to catch the exercise bug. I found that once I started to see the benefits like looking more toned and fitter, then I became more motivated. Now exercise is very much a part of my daily routine. This took time to build up. If you are starting out, exercise a couple of times a week and see how it goes.

Again use the 100% commitment rule – make a commitment to yourself for how long you will exercise on a weekly basis. Try 30 minutes, 3 times a week or whatever works best for you.

Note
- Start slow and build up gradually and you are much more likely to be in it for the longer-term.
- Make sure you keep yourself hydrated when exercising.
- Find some friends to join you and you may be more likely to support one and other.
- Try to find fun activities so that exercising can become an enjoyable part of your life.
- It might be worthwhile recording your results which might motivate you to keep going.
- Reward yourself with your results, treat yourself to massage or whatever you fancy.

Exercise
- Identify what limiting beliefs that you have that are stopping you from keeping

your body fit and healthy. Take steps to change them.
- Create space in your life for frequent exercise. Life is very busy so you may have to make some adjustments to fit exercise in to your life.
- Find exercise that you preferably enjoy and that you will be more likely to continue. Try out new things when the opportunity comes and you might just surprise yourself.
- Persevere! The first couple of months can be a challenge especially when you are not seeing the immediate results. Stop expecting instant gratification. After a few months of regular exercise, you will more than likely feel a huge difference in your energy levels.

Notes Page

How did you get on?

Your Comments

Signature _____ Date_____

Action Points

Signature _____ Date _____

"If we could give every individual the right amount of nourishment and exercise, not too little and not too much, we would have found the safest way to health."
Hippocrates

5) Rest and Relaxation

Some of you don't do enough of this and some do far too much of it.

Balance is the key.

You want to rest enough to allow your body to recover and to give you more energy to create positive experiences. However, too much R&R can leave you feeling lethargic and lacking in motivation.

It is important to regularly plan in activities that you know help you switch off. Switching off from work and from life, can give you a renewed focus. Some of the best ideas and inspiration come when you least expect it, often when you are not thinking about the job at hand.

There is not a universal way to relax – do what works best for you. Maybe you find climbing mountains is relaxing. Or maybe a massage soothes your soul. Here are a few things that are important:

Sleep – your body needs enough sleep to be able to function properly. A lack of sleep is harmful to your health and wellbeing. Sleep deprivation is the worst kind of torture as anyone who has experienced insomnia knows. A lack of sleep can make you more emotional, upset, angry and frustrated. After all, ultimately, you want to be able to enjoy your life.

Bodywork – Bodywork is a term used to describe any kind of alternative, holistic or therapeutic treatment or technique aimed at healing the body. This can include a whole host of applied disciplines including Chiropractic, Yoga, Reiki, Kinesiology, Alexander Technique, Aromatherapy Massage to name a few. These therapies are great if you are experiencing aches, pain and discomfort but also for relaxation purposes.

Laughter – It has been scientifically proven that laughter is both preventative and therapeutic in health. Laughter can help you to manage your stress better, give you a more positive outlook on life and help you to feel more energised. Remember the story of Norman Cousins?

Note
- Have a regular sleep routine by getting up at the same time on a daily basis and being sensible about any naps you may have.
- Try to get as much exposure to natural day light as possible during the day – this helps to your body to distinguish from day and night.
- Make sure that your sleep environment is relaxed and comfortable. You can improve the quality of your sleep by making sure that the room is dark, quiet, clean bedding and if possible some fresh air.
- Making improvements to your diet and to your exercise routine will make a big difference to the quality of your sleep.
- Manage your stress and anxiety levels as previously discussed as stress and anxiety can be a major contributor to lack of sleep.
- Be open and receptive to alternative approaches to your health.
- Alternative, holistic and therapeutic techniques can be a compliment to modern medicine (does not replace it).
- Research the various techniques that are available to improve your health.

- Always use a recommended or reliable provider (some techniques can be powerful so it is best to go to a trusted therapist).
- Become more aware of what, where and with whom you spend your time. Is it making you feel good?
- Watch or read things that make you feel good (avoid anything depressing!).
- Spend time with family and friends that make you laugh.
- If the last thing you feel like doing is laughing then think about giving Laughter Yoga a go! Laughter Yoga does not rely on humour or jokes so you will be able to partake even if you are not feeling too good. Laughter Yoga classes take place globally.

Exercise
- Put in place things in the evenings that will help you to unwind and de-stress. Take a bath, read a book and try to avoid anything that is distressing or upsetting on the TV, news or papers.

- Think and make a note of with whom you are spending your time with? Do the people in your life make you feel good? Can you laugh with them? It does not mean you need to cut people out of your life completely, however become more aware of your time with people that do not make you feel good.
- What do you do in your life? Is it bringing you happiness? If not, why not? It is never too late to make changes from simple everyday lifestyle choices to more important life purpose decisions. Make a list of things that you would like to change and start working on it.
- Do you have hobbies and interests that are fun and enjoyable? Give something new a try, even if it's something you only do occasionally.

Notes Page

How did you get on?

Your Comments

Signature _____ Date _____

Action Points

Signature _____ Date _____

"There is no need to go to India or anywhere else to find peace. You will find that deep place of silence right in your room, your garden or even your bathtub."
Elizabeth Kubler-Ross

4
Building Self Confidence and Self Esteem

This will help you to:
1. Identify where you need to take responsibility in your life
2. Develop the ability to follow your intuition
3. Become aware of the support that you need
4. Recognise your past successes
5. To create purpose in your life

All of the techniques described in the sections on mindfulness and building physical strength will help to build your confidence and self esteem. Better control of your thoughts, managing your emotions, improving your physical health, eliminating stress, relaxation are all about taking excellent care of yourself.

As you learn to take excellent care of yourself your confidence will naturally and gradually increase.

When you feel stronger mentally, physically and emotionally you can develop your confidence even further. The exercises in this section may help you. There is no point putting yourself under any pressure to make changes in your life.

We change when we are ready to do so, not a moment before. The main goal of this guide is to help alleviate extreme distress and pressure. It is not intended to add any more pressure to your life. Therefore, only use if and when you feel ready.

1) Taking Responsibility

You are responsible for your life. Every decision you have made has led you to where you are now. This does not mean that you start blaming yourself for everything, especially the bad decisions. This will not achieve anything and certainly not build self esteem.

Instead, check how do you avoid taking responsibility? Do you use any one of the resistance techniques already described in Section 1:

- Denial
- Blaming ourselves or others
- Diversion

- Over indulgence in food or alcohol
- Taking drugs to numb emotions
- Becoming dependent on other people

When you are suffering from extreme stress, anxiety or depression you are offered a 'get out of jail free card' or so you think. The option is there for you to accept the theory that your difficulties are caused by a brain disease. There are many people preaching this theory. You can put your hands up and say, "It's not my fault." and family members can do the same. You might receive the love and affection that you desperately need.

However good this may feel in the short-term there is a major drawback longer-term. If you believe that there are outside forces controlling your life including your health then you give away your power.

When you feel like you are not in control of your own life, you lose strength. As a result your self confidence and esteem will plummet. Dependencies and self destructive behaviours will get worse. It is a vicious cycle.

This is a large price to pay!

How do you avoid taking responsibility of your life?

How do you move forward and take responsibility?

- Make conscious decisions – every moment, you are making decisions – what to wear, what to eat, who to spend time with. In many cases you are not thinking about what is best for the longer-term. You are more concerned with instant gratification – feeling good, NOW. Longer-term health and happiness is largely dependant on your ability to make better conscious decisions in the present moment. You have to learn to ask yourself the right questions. "What is the potential outcome of my decision? How is this going to make me feel?"

Spend some time thinking about the decisions that you have made. How has it led you to where you are now?

- Get focused – to make better decisions you must know what it is you are trying to achieve. You can down download the free 'Lifestyle Profile' questionnaire at *www.life-is-now.co.uk*. This will help you to focus where you are at the moment. If you are distressed and suffering the results of excess stress then it if likely that your current priority will be your health and wellbeing.

Make a note of what your key priorities are? What is your focus?

- Be prepared to learn – the reason that you have made the decisions that you have is because you did not know any better. You don't know what you don't know. The way that you improve the decisions you make is through learning. . You need to make sure that you learn from those "who know". By this I mean there are many people out there who preach how to do things without ever doing it themselves. The best teachers and leaders are those who are living breathing examples of what they teach.

It is easy to access knowledge and it is affordable. There are lots of sources detailed in Section 5 of this guide. You have access to the local library. Most of the best teachers have shared their life learning through books. Make sure that you choose people who have similar values to yourself. Who can you learn from?

Notes Page

How did you get on?

Your Comments

Signature _____ Date _____

Action Points

Signature _____ Date _____

"Most people do not really want freedom, because freedom involves responsibility, and most people are frightened of responsibility."
Sigmund Freud

2) Follow Your Intuition

Your intuition is your internal GPS. Your thoughts and feelings are there to keep you on track. Dismissing them is detrimental to your health and well being. When you feel good, you will be more in tune with what's going on inside of you.

I have already said that the journey from the head to the heart is not an easy one. However, undoubtedly that it is the most rewarding one. More love, peace, fulfillment, gratefulness and compassion – who wouldn't want more of that? The benefits far outweigh the challenges.

It will take courage and strength to follow your own heart. Remember, it is easier to live the life that others expect of you. It is easy to look for approval from those close to you – those whom you have been brought up to respect. Also remember it is the fastest road to unhappiness and ill-health.

It will require a dedication to the truth at all costs – the truth in your eyes. I have already talked about the fact that the truth can sometimes hurt. I have also talked about how you can learn to accept and work through the natural growth process when these times come. The other option is to resist and deny the truth. Only you can decide whether that is how you want to live your life. Is it worth the sacrifice?

If you choose to follow your heart, be prepared to meet resistance head on. You read the list Steven Pressfield identified as the biggest hits for resistance. When you embark on anything that is going to be good for you to help you grow, you will likely find resistance.

How do we beat resistance?

1) **Clarity** – Be very clear about what you want. If you don't know where you are going, it will be hard to reach the destination. Complete the 'Lifestyle Profile' (download from *www.life-is-now.co.uk*) questionnaire to figure out your starting point. Be clear about the end result that you are aiming for. Lack of decision will leave you stuck. Lack of decision also allows room for fear and

doubt to enter your mind. Resistance will love this.

2) **Plan** – Make a plan as to how you can achieve what you are aiming to do. Do you know how to get there? If not, source people that have achieved what you want. Learn from them and create your own plan. If you don't have a plan, again resistance will step in if given the opportunity.

3) **Action** – take daily action to take you nearer to your goals. You need to take action to determine whether it feels right or not. It can be easy to say that you are waiting for an intuitive nudge, sometimes these come but sometimes not. When you start something new and learn more of 'what not to do', this is normal. To learn new skills you will go through a corrective process until you feel confident. If you are doing something that does not feel right, trust your feelings and go back to the plan – it might be time to amend. It is no use spending time doing visualisations and affirmations described in 'Heal Your Mind' if you don't take daily action too.

4) **Be brave** – don't confuse intuitive feelings with fear. Whilst I have established that fear does not exist in reality, it feels very real indeed. You have to be prepared to

take continuous and repetitive action to face our fears. Repeat the tasks that scare you until you have desensitised yourself to the event. I have done this a number of times to overcome – fear of driving long distances, fear of flying, fear of interviews and fear of public speaking. If you do something enough times you effectively re-train your subconscious mind. You can start enjoying activities you once feared. This will require you to have unwavering faith that things will work out for the best – especially when you meet with temporary defeat. You will on occasions meet with disappointments, this is to be expected.

Notes Page

How did you get on?

Your Comments

Signature _____ Date _____

Action Points

Signature _____ Date _____

"Listen to your intuition. It will tell you everything you need to know."
Anthony J. D'Angelo

3) Build a Cheerleading Team

When you decide to take responsibility for your own life it is vital to have a support network, not to lean on, for your purpose is to find your own inner strength but simply to be there for you. I didn't always have the support network that I have now. This is largely because I did not have the right people in my life.

Choice
When you become more aware you realise that you may not have made the best choices with regards to your friends. You may also be entangled in unhealthy family relationships. Neither of these is conducive to your health and happiness. The path of personal growth requires that you make decisions to bring peace and harmony to these relationships.

This has been one of my biggest personal challenges. Once I overcame my difficulties with stress and anxiety, I developed confidence in my own ability to grow and help myself. This is when I became interested in personal development. Today, my support network looks drastically different to what it did then. It is my personal belief that this happens to many people on the self improvement path.

As you grow, you effectively change. Your personality remains but you become a better version of yourself. You change on the inside. You become more aware and start to see things much more clearly. You become more conscious of the consequences of your actions: cause and effect. Ultimately, you start to take more control of your life, rather than letting it take control of you.

Changes in your inner world will have a knock on effect on your outer world. Sometimes the changes will seem radical and other times not. Some people will like the changes and differences in you and some will not.

The people who continue to support you in growth, and continue to have a positive influence in your life, are likely to be around longer term. I have a few friends that have remained steadfastly in my life through these times and I would say that these relationships have strengthened as a result. In my opinion their light has shone brightly and they have been unwavering in their support. My changing has not threatened them in any way.

Resistance
There are other people who don't particularly like change. They feel safe and secure when everything stays the same. Change scares them. You may feel the effects of this in the form of negativity, criticism, blame, anger and a whole host of other negative emotions. Often the negative feelings will be subtle. This might be a feeling that you pick up from the other person – the way they look or speak to you.

This has brought disappointment on occasions, especially with one friend whom had been a particularly close friend since meeting in college. When I look at the closeness of the relationship and the length of time it lasted, I can hardly believe was has happened to our friendship in the past couple of years. I rarely see this friend now and often when we meet the relationship feels strained.

Relationships are complex and we don't necessarily understand why relationships change. We often don't see things from the other person's point of view. We may be willing to look at the other person's perspective but it does not mean that they are willing to do the same. We can only work and improve on our own interactions. We cannot control the actions of anyone else.

Expectations
Friendships end is because of expectations. When you put expectations on other people, or when people put certain expectations on you, I believe, there is always room for disappointment. It can be hard to live up to expectations.

Removing expectations and allowing the people around you room to be themselves, their true colours shine through.

Those that have unnecessary expectations of you will likely leave your life or the relationship will drastically change and contact diminish. As sad as this may be, there is definitely a positive side to this. When people leave your life, you create the space for new people to enter.

I have really enjoyed this experience over the past few years. I have met new people that have enriched my life in many ways. We attract people into our lives that are of a similar mindset to ourselves. People who reflect back to us our thoughts and beliefs.

You need to surround yourself with people that make you feel good about yourself. People who can let you be yourself and offer you the support and encouragement that you need. My own experience tells me that true friends will be there with you during the good and bad times.

True friends are there for you when the bad times come; all of the others are really only acquaintances. It also takes a true friend to celebrate the good times, to be genuinely happy for you when things are going well.

So my final thoughts are that it is crucial to choose your friends wisely.

Take some time and think about the people in your life. Who do you feel good with after spending time with them? Who does not make you feel good? Start to become more aware of who you spend your time with.

Notes Page

How did you get on?

```
Your Comments



Signature _____ Date _____
```

```
Action Points



Signature _____ Date _____
```

"Don't walk behind me; I may not lead. Don't walk in front of me; I may not follow. Just walk beside me and be my friend".
Albert Camus

4) Learning to say NO.

Developing the confidence to say no is one of the most powerful actions that you can take to build your self esteem.

Your time, health and wellbeing are extremely precious. Saying yes to please and help others all the time can be seriously detrimental to your own development.

If you don't treat yourself with the upmost respect, how can you expect more from other people? You need to learn to put yourself and your needs first. This is even the case when you have children. One of the biggest gifts you can teach your children is that of self respect.

Rather than this being as selfish as it might sound, the opposite is true. When you fill yourself up with love and joy the consequence is that you have much more to give to those you love.

The difference being that you are not giving from a place of resentment, frustration and negativity. You are able to give because you have so much more to give. Your giving does not deplete your energy but conversely gives you more energy.

Complete the following exercise ....

It is time to have a heart to heart with yourself. Where are you putting others needs before your own? Where are you giving your time out of obligation? What activities are you involved with that you wish you weren't? What are the things that you don't enjoy doing? Who do you need to start saying NO to?

5) Celebrate Past Successes

Another excellent way to build confidence is to acknowledge all of your past successes. When you are feeling low, you are more focused on failures. Don't forget that you also have had many successes through out your life.

I bet if I were to ask you to share your failures, you could quickly tell me how many times you have messed up in the last month. If I asked you to tell me how many successes you have had, you would struggle. Am I right?

When you feel low about yourself it is critical that you recognise and celebrate any improvements that you make. You must build on your successes one step at a time, no matter how small.

Otherwise, you stay in that low rut longer. Frankly, if you are not willing to take any risks to build yourself up, any possibility of rejection or failure becomes too much to bear. The sooner and the more you can build your self confidence and esteem the sooner and more risks you will be willing to take. People that have very high esteem can take rejection and failure hand in hand. This is something to strive for.

If you recognise and accept that you have had success in the past, you will be more likely to believe that you can have successes again in the future.

Try some of these exercises –

- List 100 successes that you have had. It will need to include even your earliest successes like learning to ride your bike or getting a part in the school play. It will be easier to begin with and then you might start to struggle but persevere. List items such as getting your first job, passing your driving test, and getting married. It's important to acknowledge them all. You may have to start listing passing each exam but keep going until you reach 100.
- Create a success journal. Use the Appendix at the end of this guide. You can keep a track of any further progress that you make.

Notes Page

How did you get on?

Your Comments

Signature _____ Date _____

Action Points

Signature _____ Date _____

> "Self-confidence is the first requisite to great undertakings."
> **Samuel Johnson**

6) Living a Life of Purpose

Despite what you may have been led to believe, life is not meant to be difficult, complex or a struggle. You have been blessed with unique talents and abilities that and are able to share for the greater good.

Stop searching for happiness and fulfilment in your outer world – money, possessions, status, careers. What are you really chasing? And what are you giving up in the process?

You may give up some freedom, time and mostly your soul for money. However, I hope that one day you will be able to retire comfortably and spend more time with those that you love. But, what if you don't live to see retirement?
This parable is the perfect example:

An American investment banker was taking a much needed vacation in a small coastal Mexican village when a small boat with just one fisherman docked. The fisherman's catch included several large, fresh fish.

The investment banker was impressed by the quality of the fish and asked the Mexican how long it took to catch them. The Mexican replied,

"Only a little while." The banker then asked why he didn't stay out longer and catch more fish?

The Mexican fisherman replied he had enough to support his family's immediate needs.

The American then asked "But what do you do with the rest of your time?"

The Mexican fisherman replied, "I sleep late, fish a little, play with my children, take siesta with my wife, stroll into the village each evening where I sip wine and play guitar with my amigos. I have a full and busy life, senor."

The investment banker scoffed, "I am an Ivy League MBA, and I could help you. You could spend more time fishing and with the proceeds buy a bigger boat, and with the proceeds from the bigger boat you could buy several boats until eventually you would have a whole fleet of fishing boats. Instead of selling your catch to the middleman you could sell directly to the processor, eventually opening your own cannery. You could control the product, processing and distribution."

Then he added, "Of course, you would need to leave this small coastal fishing village and move to Mexico City where you would run your growing enterprise."

The Mexican fisherman asked, "But senor, how long will this all take?"

To which the American replied, "Fifteen to twenty years."

"But what then?" asked the Mexican.

The American laughed and said, "That's the best part. When the time is right you would announce an IPO and sell your company stock to the public and become very rich. You could make millions."

"Millions, senor? Then what?"

To which the investment banker replied, "Then you would retire. You could move to a small coastal fishing village where you would sleep late, fish a little, play with your kids, take siesta with your wife, stroll to the village in the evenings where you could sip wine and play your guitar with your amigos."

I think you know where I'm going with this story.

Would you like to find out more about yourself? Spend your time doing things that you love and learning how you can be financially rewarded in the process?

Take your time to go through each of the following questions and make notes. Make sure that you have peace and quiet and that you are in a positive frame of mind.

1) If you didn't need to worry about money, what would you do all day long?
2) What are your favourite activities? When do you lose track of time?
3) Who do you love spending time with most? What qualities and values do the people you enjoy possess?
4) What makes you feel good about yourself?
5) What are your greatest strengths/qualities? If you are not sure, ask someone close to you to give you an honest opinion.
6) What message do you have to share with others? What makes you angry or puts a fire in your belly? What would you like to change?
7) What do you value most in life?
8) Who is your biggest inspiration? What do they do or what message do they share that you strongly admire?
9) Fast forward to the future, you are on your death bed and reflecting on your life.

What has been the important thing that you have accomplished and achieved? What has been the most important relationships? What has been your biggest priority?

Notes Page

_____

_____

_____

_____

_____

_____

_____

_____

_____

_____

_____

_____

_____

The Roadmap Exercise

By understanding your past decisions you will have a better understanding of your values and what's important to you. It will give you a far deeper insight into your motivations. You can do the analysis yourself by answering the questions below or you can have someone interview you. A partner can help you to see any patterns in your decision making.

Your partner does not need to be a professional. You can provide them with the questions in the following pages. All you need is for them to give you their time and interest.

For each choice that you made, figure out the reason WHY. The patterns may reveal themselves gradually as you answer why you made each decision.

Here are the questions:

Education
Where did you go to college or university? What was the reason for your choice?

What did you qualify in?

First Job/First Life Event
What was your first proper job/life event? What were you looking for in this? Why did you make the choice that you made?

What were your long-term goals as you started your career?

How did this work out in terms of your goals?

What were the most important things you learned on your first job/life event?

Next Job/Life Event (Ask the next 4 questions for each change in job or life circumstances)
What was your next job/life event? What brought this about? Why did you move?

How did this work out in terms of your goals?

What were the most important things you learned in this job/life change?

What was the next job change or life event? Why did it occur?

Review

As you look back on your life, do you see any major turning points? What were they and why did they occur?

What were some of the things that you enjoying in your life so far?

What were some of the things that you did not enjoy and would like to avoid in the future? Why?

In what way have your ambitions changed? What do you see now as your long-term goals?

What is the ultimate job that you would like to have?

What are your major strengths?

What are some critical values that guide your choice in jobs/life?

Do you see any patterns?

Living a life of purpose requires a greater understanding of yourself, your strengths and how you can use them for the greater good. Use the following notes pages to write any ideas or thoughts that you may have.

Notes Page

How did you get on?

Your Comments

Signature _____ Date _____

Action Points

Signature _____ Date _____

"When I chased after money, I never had enough. When I got my life on purpose and focused on giving of myself and everything that arrived into my life, then I was prosperous."
Wayne Dyer

5
Additional Sources of Help

Objectives
This will help you:
1. Identify who you should listen to
2. Build awareness of the various support options available (including different approaches to counselling, therapy and alternative therapies)
3. Understand sources of further information.

Who Should You Listen To?

It's easier when you are feeling vulnerable and unsure in which direction to take to seek the advice of others. And quite frankly, they will happily give us their opinions. People love to feel needed and love to be right! However, how helpful is this for you?

Most of the time, this only hinders progress. I talked about the need to listen to your own thoughts and feelings as a driving force for moving forward. When you ask family or friends for their opinion, the majority of time you are not seeking advice but their approval.

The need for approval and love is deep rooted and can be traced back to childhood. You will continue to seek this love and approval from those close to you unless you do something about it.

If you want to grow and develop, you must accept the notion that you don't need anyone's approval. In fact if you change and start to follow your heart rather than your head, you are going to ruffle a few feathers. The people around you won't know what hit them!

The need for approval stunts growth. In his book, *Psycho-Cybernetics*, Maxwell Maltz provides the perfect illustration for this. He asks you to think of yourself going to these people with a begging bowl and begging for money. Would you do it? Of course not, so why do you feel the need to do the same for approval. That is effectively what you are doing.

The point I am making is this; think carefully and wisely before you seek council from others. Of course you need support and guidance. It's a natural part of growing. You are human and need interaction and encouragement. However, not everyone will have your best interests at heart. It can be hard to know the true motives of others. Time usually reveals peoples true colours.

Who are the people that you are taught to respect and listen to?
- Parents
- Teachers
- Elders
- Religious leaders
- Medical professionals
- Most other 'professionals'

So far, my life experience has taught me to question anyone's learning that has come through education alone. Real learning comes through personal experience. Real leaders are those that are living and breathing examples of what they teach.

My experience has also taught me that the majority of the life teachers listed above are not living and breathing examples of what they preach. The most successful change leaders are successful for a reason. They are authentic, genuine and transparent - their true colours shine very brightly. They attract people like a magnet.

There is a story about Ghandi which highlights this notion.

A woman took her son to see Ghandi and she asked him to tell her son to stop eating sugar because it was ruining his health. Ghandi said to her to come back in one month. When they returned Ghandi told the boy to stop eating sugar because it was ruining his health. The woman asked Ghandi why they had waited a month. Ghandi replied, "One month ago I was still eating sugar!"

In my opinion this is one of the biggest failings of many leaders and many people within the health profession. How many times have you been to see an over-weight unhealthy looking GP who is telling you to eat healthily and exercise! There is nothing inspiring or authentic about that.

To get the best support and advice you need to:

1. Be very clear about what you are looking to achieve.
2. Find someone that has successfully achieved what you want. Make sure that they closely match your values.
3. Listen carefully to what they have to say. You don't need to have the money for coaching or mentoring. The majority of these people will have made it easy for you to access their ideas and route to success.
4. Take on board what resonates and try some of the success principles to see if they work for you. Only do what feels right. Remember this is your life you are creating and not a carbon copy of another's.

Support to Change

Therapy/Counselling

Counselling or therapy is a very good option if you are clear about the exact reasons that you are going. If you are going to explore your limiting beliefs and emotional baggage in order to move on with your life, then it can be a positive experience. Counsellors and therapists are trained to help release baggage. Make sure you find one who has been through the process personally. All of them have had to face their own limiting beliefs and emotional baggage to understand and help you to do the same. Counselling and therapy can help you to come to terms with the past. Be aware not to become stuck in the past and in therapeutic relationships for way longer than you need. It is easy to become dependent on counsellors or therapists. The main Approaches to Counselling/therapy:

- **Cognitive Behavioural Therapy**
    - A form of psychotherapy.
    - It is the leading approach in the UK for many recognised conditions of emotional distress – anxiety, depression, panic, phobias, post traumatic stress disorder.

- It is based on a 5 factor model on how you experience the world. You respond to the world through your thoughts, feelings, emotions, behaviours and physiology.
- It will challenge your thoughts and thinking.
- The focus is on the here/now and the future. It will consider past conditioning for current decision making.
- High level of involvement – clients are given homework to complete.

- **Person Centred Counselling**
    - Talking therapy developed by Psychologist, Carl Rogers in the 40's/50's.
    - Non-directive approach that believes in the client's potential and ability to make the right choices for themselves regardless of the therapist's values, ideas and beliefs.
    - The counsellor provides the environment for this to take place –

congruence, empathy and
unconditional positive regard.
- **Gestalt**
  - Developed by Fritz Perls, German Psychiatrist and Psychotherapist.
  - Focus is on increasing awareness of sensations, perceptions, bodily feelings and emotions in the present moment – paying attention to the NOW, listen to the messages and take action.
  - Relationship is of high importance along with contact with the environment.
  - Most effectively used in groups.
- **Psychoanalysis**
  - Longer-term process.
  - Talking therapy which aims to give you a deeper understanding of your problems/challenges.
  - Therapy focuses on the past in relation to current problems/challenges.
  - Can be used individually or in a group.

Deciding Which Type of Therapy
Consider the following:

1) How collaborative do you want the process to be?

   Is it a journey that you want to go on by yourself or do you want it to be a collaborative process. Person centred and Gestalt is about "you". CBT is more collaborative and it's a joint process.

2) Are you psychologically minded?

   To be able to challenge your thoughts and thinking you need to be psychologically minded. You need to be able to have a basic understanding of the theory to engage in CBT. This approach is not for everyone and if this is challenging for you, another approach to therapy is recommended.

3) What is your motivation for involvement?

Are you looking for a focused approach (CBT)? Do you want to do homework out with therapy sessions? Or would you prefer a less direct method?

4) What is accessible?

What therapy/counselling is accessible to you? You might like the sound of Gestalt therapy but are there Gestalt therapists in your area? You might also want to consider cost. If you are unable to pay for qualified therapists or counsellors, you will always be able to find students that are looking for clients.

Personal Development/Self Help

Ask yourself, do you dismiss self help and personal development as a sign of weakness? Would you be embarrassed to be found browsing the self help aisle in the book shop? The truth of the matter is these self help authors are the TOP leaders in change and transformation. Not only have they achieved it themselves, some are teaching it to millions of others.

They have learned self mastery – they have all managed to get past their limiting beliefs and emotional baggage and they have all re-programmed their subconscious mind. The majority of these books tell you how to do this. Once you have read a number of them you realise that they are all teaching you the same thing, only said in unique and different ways.

Louise Hay, Jack Canfield, Napoleon Hill, Joe Vitale, Jim Rohn, Brian Tracy, Dale Carnegie, Bob Proctor, Steven Covey – have inspired change and growth in more people than anyone in the medical profession. Inspirational leaders focus their attention and others on what they want to grow – health, confidence, abundance, happiness.

They all understand the power of the mind. Every single one of them also understands that thoughts and beliefs affect the body and what we experience physically. They all understand that health underpins growth. In fact I would go as far to say that health (mentally and physically) is the foundation for change and growth. As we have seen poor mental health is the often the result of resisting personal growth.

Alternatives

There are a number of alternative health practices which can help to get past the mind and work with you on an energetic level. If this is too much for your mind to accept then choose something that resonates with you. If you are open minded , here are a number of options:

- Emotional Freedom Techniques
- Acupuncture
- Homeopathy
- Reiki
- Hypnotherapy
- Acupuncture
- Indian Head Massage
- Craniosacral Therapy
- NLP (neuro-linguistic programming)
- Energy medicine
- Kinesiology
- Spiritual Response Therapy

Before you dismiss this as a load of codswallop, understand this. We are highly influenced by the media in our lives. We may believe that alterative health approaches are a waste of time. They may not provide the instant gratification that we look for when we seek help from traditional medicine.

The ONLY reason that there are not more studies into the effectiveness of alternative health is because there is no money to be made by this research. Who is going to fund trials and research in this? The majority of drug trials are funded by drug companies -the most lucrative industry in the whole world.

I love Kinesiology and Spiritual Response Therapy (I go to an excellent practitioner). This has proved to be more effective and powerful than anything else that I have tried. However it raises a few eyebrows. ☺

> "A leader is one who knows the way, goes the way, and shows the way".
> **John Maxwell**

Sources of Further Information

Abortion Help
0845 300 80 90
24-hour abortion information service run by Marie Stopes International clinics.

Age UK
0800 00 99 66
Information and advice on a broad rance of topics affecting older people

Alcoholics Anonymous
0845 769 7555
For those who think their drinking is becoming a problem, Alcoholics Anonymous offers the chance to talk to someone who knows the issues through personal experience.

Beating Eating Disorders
0845 634 1414
Confidential helpline offering support and advice for anyone affected by an eating disorder.

Beaumont Society
01582 412220
Advice and support for transgender, transvestite, transsexual and crossdressing people to reduce emotional stress and increase understanding.

Breast Cancer Care helpline
0808 800 6000
Nurses and trained workers with personal or professional experience of breast cancer offer information and support on any aspect of breast cancer or breast health.

Cancerbackup
0808 800 1234
Information from nurses about all types and aspects of cancer - diagnosis, treatment, symptom control, clinical trials, support groups and where to get practical and emotional help.

Carers Direct
0808 802 0202

Confidential information and advice for anyone looking after someone else.

Contact a Family
0808 808 3555
Information on specific conditions and rare disorders for families with disabled children.

Crohn's and Colitis Support
0845 130 3344
A confidential, supportive listening service provided by trained volunteers for anyone affected by inflammatory bowel disease (IBD). Lines are open weekdays 1pm-3.30pm and 6.30pm-9pm

Crohn's and Colitis UK
0845 130 2233
An information service for people affected by inflammatory bowel disease (IBD). Calls are taken by Information Officers from 10am-1pm weekdays. An answering service operates at other times.

Cruse Day by Day
0844 477 9400
Help and support for people who are bereaved. Also offers a special line for young people on 0808 808 1677.

Domestic Violence Helpline
0808 2000 247
National Domestic Violence 24-hour helpline for those who require an urgent response or need in-depth support. The helpline is run by Women's Aid and Refuge.

Drinkline
0800 917 8282
Information and self-help materials, help to callers worried about their own drinking, support for family and friends of people who are drinking, and advice on where to go for help.

FPA
0845 122 8690
For information and advice on contraception, sexually transmitted infections, pregnancy choices, abortion, or planning a pregnancy

Frank
0800 77 66 00

Call for confidential and friendly advice about drugs from professional advisers who will give you straight up, unbiased information.

Hearing Voices Network
0114 271 8210
For people who hear voices, see visions or have other unusual perceptions.

Heart helpline
08450 70 80 70
British Heart Foundation's cardiac nurses and information officers provide information to help support any medical advice you have already had from your GP or consultant.

Learning Disability Helpline
0808 808 1111
An advice and information service from Mencap for people with a learning disability, their families and carers.

Macmillan CancerLine
0808 808 2020
Information and advice for anyone with concerns about living with cancer. Also offers a textphone service on 0808 808 0121.

Meningitis Research Foundation
0808 800 3344
Trained staff and qualified nurses offer information on meningitis and septicaemia to anyone concerned about or affected by these infections.

Mind Info Line
0300 123 3393
Mind's helpline gives confidential advice and help for people with mental health problems

NHS Direct
0845 4647
Health advice, information and reassurance, 24 hours a day, 365 days a year.

Rethink
0845 456 0455
Helpline services offering practical and emotional support to those experiencing severe mental illness, their carers and relatives.

Sexual health line
0800 567123

Free confidential information and advice on sexual health

Shelter
0808 800 4444
Free housing advice from the homelessness and housing charity.

Stroke helpline
0845 303 3100
Advice from the Stroke Association, which helps stroke patients and their families through its support services and funds research into prevention, treatment and rehabilitation.

The Samaritans
08457 90 90 90
Confidential non-judgemental emotional support, 24 hours a day, for people who feel distressed, despairing or suicidal.

THT Direct
0845 1221 200
Information, support and advice from the Terrence Higgins Trust on all aspects of HIV and sexual health

Appendix

Night time tips

The evenings can be challenging especially if the time you use to chill out. It will become more apparent to you that you are not able to do the same. In the meantime, begin to create a healthy and calming evening routine.

Also if you have young children then the sooner you get them in to a bedtime routine the better. Bedtime routines are advantageous for children as is having enough sleep. This will also give you your evenings to yourself.

If you have a partner, make sure that they read the tips for partner's information. In the meantime, accept that the evenings are going to be your time. This is time for you to do what you need to, to get yourself well again. This is not a time for you to feel guilty for taking time to yourself. Your health has to be the number one priority at the moment. You are of no use to anyone else when you are feeling highly stressed and anxious. So take the time, and do what you need to do, guilt free.

- ✓ Make sure that you have had an evening meal or supper and that any snacks are healthy. Try a piece of fruit or some nuts.
- ✓ Avoid all caffeine – no fizzy drinks, no coffee and no tea.
- ✓ Avoid alcohol – not forever ☺ but until you are well again!
- ✓ Turn the TV off or go to another room!
- ✓ If you enjoy a hot bath you could have this with relaxing music and some candles.
- ✓ Engage in an activity that will require your attention (diversion) or if you feel able do some light exercise – yoga (I recommend Maya Fiennes Kundalini Yoga). Alternatively, you could do a guided visualisation. Try out some different things and then do what works best for you.
- ✓ Write your affirmations out 10 – 20 times – remember say them with feeling as you write.
- ✓ Write your daily gratitude diary – you could do this somewhere very comfortable with relaxing music.
- ✓ Prepare a short list of the actions that you want to complete for tomorrow. Make

sure that you have at least 3 and no more than 6. Break these down so they are achievable. We want to keep a focus for the day but by no means do you want to add anymore stress or anxiety to your full life. One action may be to simply make a phone call that you have been putting off or you may want to book an alternative therapy treatment. It would be a good idea to make sure that these actions are positive actions that are going to help you on the road to recovery.
- ✓ Review your activities list for today and congratulate yourself for achieving them. (see the 30 day planner)
- ✓ Have a regular bedtime – remember you want to establish a routine and get 7 to 8 hours sleep per night.
- ✓ Lights out and sleep and remember you can STOP those thoughts of "not sleeping"
- ✓ Be patient. Keep going and with practice and consistency, it will get better and easier.

"Never, never, never give up."
Winston Churchill

Morning Tips

Today is a new day and you are going to keep moving forward no matter how tough it gets! Stress, anxiety and depression are often at their worst when you first wake up in the morning. This is because you go from a state of sleep straight in to an anxious state. This is such a big contrast.

There are a number of things that you can do before you start your day off.

- ✓ If mornings are busy for you and you have get ready, ready your family, to go to work you would set the alarm half an hour earlier.
- ✓ Take a quick look over your daily planner – make sure you know what your focus is for the day.
- ✓ You might want to write out your affirmations and get your mind prepared for the day ahead.
- ✓ The morning is a great time to exercise and move your body. This can increase your energy levels and get you moving.

- ✓ If you have time, do a guided visualisation or a form of meditation.
- ✓ Read through the Mind tools and techniques again and make sure that you know all the exercises that you can be doing through-out the day to train your mind.
- ✓ Have a substantial and healthy breakfast. People often miss breakfast but it is one of the most important meals of the day. You need to make sure that you are putting the fuel in that you need. (e.g. oats, muesli, fresh fruit)

Rather than tell yourself that you are going to have a terrible day, try telling yourself that today is going to be a good day.

> "You are successful the moment you start moving toward a worthwhile goal."
> **Chuck Carlson**

Panic Attack Tips

There is a way to quickly stop panic attacks, and that is because no matter how bad the experience is **YOU** have the power to stop it. Remember the attack is brought on by the thoughts you are having. You will probably not even be aware of the thoughts you are having until you are slap bang in the middle of an attack.

Also remember the thoughts you are having are increasing the adrenalin in your blood and causing a physical affect in your body. Once you start to experience the physical affects, heart racing, blurred vision, chest pains and all the other horrible sensations, your thoughts then spiral out of control. "Oh my God! I am going to die! Something terrible is going to happen!" You know it can be a quick downward spiral.

As soon as you become aware that you are having a panic attack:
- Take control of the situation. It may be tempting to make a run for it. ☺ Go back home or to somewhere 'safe'. But the thing is anxiety tends to follow you wherever you go, so soon you won't feel safe there either.

- Do not fight or run from the symptoms, the key is to ACCEPT what you are feeling.
- Understand that you can come to no harm at all. The sensations you feel in your body are a result of the thoughts that you have been having and the increased adrenalin levels. Your body is reacting normally to the flight or fight response. To stop the sensations your adrenalin levels need to return to a "normal" level.
- Breathe, breathe, breathe! Count your breathing until you feel able to carry on for the time that it takes to return to a more relaxed state.
- Remember and become the watcher of your thoughts. It is this that will give you power and control over your life.
- Consciously choose your thoughts and say affirmations, "I am calm and at peace.", "I am safe and well.", or whatever works best for you. Say it over and over again, and say it with feeling. Choose thoughts that will nurture as opposed to thoughts that are going to keep you in a downward spiral.

- Think carefully about the words that you speak. It may be tempting to tell people and talk to people about the anxiety attack. However, you will only be adding to what you are experiencing and attracting more of this to you.
- Also think carefully about the actions that you take. The anxious mind will want to change the way you behave. You will want to start adapting certain things that you do, you will want to analyse the situation, research it, and visit every professional that you can.
- Once you have stopped the attack, you should carry on normal life as quickly as possible and forget the panic attack. Try not to analyse it, talk about it or act differently as this is the quickest way to move forward.

Make the decision NOW. Stop the panic attack as fast as it starts!

> "Listen to what you know instead of what you fear."
> **RICHARD BACH**

Tips for Partner and Family

If your partner or close family member is suffering from extreme stress or anxiety, I appreciate it can be difficult for you to understand what is going on for them. I also understand that it can also be incredibly frustrating that you do not know what you can do to help.

- ✓ Read through this book and make sure that you know what the symptoms are and also the reason why people experience stress, anxiety and depression.
- ✓ Help your partner/family member to identify the ways that they have changed and adapted their behaviour since suffering from excess stress.
- ✓ Gently remind your partner when you notice them talking about their symptoms or when they continue to adapt their behaviour – the sooner they stop, the quicker the symptoms will disappear. If they are struggling, you can comfort/hold their hand, to let them know that you are

there. However, this is their fight, not yours.
- ✓ Encourage your partner to communicate and express emotions. Just because you don't talk about the symptoms does not mean you stop communication about everything else.
- ✓ Encourage and help your partner to use affirmations. These are really important and results can be quite quick. So write them on post-it notes and place them in places that they will see them. Get involved with the affirmations. This is a great way to show your love, support and understanding. The point is to say affirmations like they are real and that you believe them.
- ✓ Help to make sure that your partner/family member is eating healthily and regularly. See the advice and help making sure that you have the right food in the house or prepare meals.
- ✓ Accept your partner/family member needs to have extra time in the morning and evenings to work on themselves. Often stress and anxiety sufferers feel

guilty for the attention that has been on them. However, taking this time is important in their recovery.

Success Journal

Recommended Reading

Byrne, Rhonda, *The Secret*

Canfield, Jack, *The Success Principles*

Chopra, Deepak, The Seven Spiritual Laws of Success

Gibran, Kahil, *The Prophet*

Hay, Louise, *You Can Heal Your Life*

Hill, Napoleon, *Think and Grow Rich*

Lynch, Terry, *Beyond Prozac*

Maltz, Maxwell, *The New Psych-Cybernetics*

Peck, Scott, *The Road Less Travelled*

Pert, Candice, *Molecules of Emotion*

Pressfield Steven, *The War of Art*

Tolle, Eckhart, *The Power of Now*

Whitaker, Robert, *Anatomy of an Epidemic*

We hope you enjoyed the book.

Sign up via the Life is Now website to receive the free Lifestyle Profile Questionnaire. You will also receive a free regular newsletter, with updates, offers and much more!

www.life-is-now.co.uk

We would love to hear from you, please send any questions or feedback to:

info@life-is-now.co.uk

Printed in Poland
by Amazon Fulfillment
Poland Sp. z o.o., Wrocław